LEADING
KIDS
to
JESUS

Other Books by David Staal

Leading Your Child to Jesus:
How Parents Can Talk with Their Kids about Faith

Making Your Children's Ministry the Best Hour
of Every Kid's Week (With Sue Miller)

LEADING KIDS to JESUS

{ how to have one-on-one conversations about faith }

DAVID STAAL

ZONDERVAN™

GRAND RAPIDS, MICHIGAN 49530 USA

WILLOW
Willow Creek Resources

ZONDERVAN.COM/
AUTHORTRACKER

ZONDERVAN™

Leading Kids to Jesus
Copyright © 2005 by Willow Creek Association

Requests for information should be addressed to:
Zondervan, *Grand Rapids, Michigan 49530*

Library of Congress Cataloging-in-Publication Data

Staal, David.
    Leading kids to Jesus : how to have one-on-one coversations about faith /
David Staal.
        p. cm.
    Includes index.
    ISBN-13: 978-0-310-26382-1 (softcover)
    ISBN-10: 0-310-26382-4 (softcover)
    1. Church work with children. 2. Evangelistic work. I. Title.
BV639.C4S68 2005
259'.22—dc22

2005013228

Interior design by Beth Shagene

Illustrations by Liz Conrad

Printed in the United States of America

---

06 07 08 09 10 11 12 • 19 18 17 16 15 14 13 12 11 10 9 8 7 6 5 4 3 2 1

Contents

To Promiseland small group leaders—
who have loved and led
thousands of kids to Jesus,
one at a time.
Thanks.

Foreword

Since the earliest days of pastoring Willow Creek Community Church, I've agonized over my sermons. Time and again, I've had to throw out first drafts and start over. Countless hours and multiple rewrites later, even the messages I delivered often left me feeling I could have done more to make this or that point a little clearer. But the second guessing I did on those communications paled by comparison to the weight that pressed down on me years ago as I pondered how to introduce Jesus to my two young children, Shauna and Todd. What was the best way to approach such critical discussions? I'll take the pressure of sermon preparation for 15,000 adults any day!

Thanks be to God, in his goodness and mercy, my children (now grown) love God, love his church, and understand grace. Apparently my fumbling attempts worked—and perhaps even more to the point, our army of Promiseland volunteers did yeoman's service for my kids (and thousands of others) by explaining and modeling God's persistent and pervasive love.

When it comes to conversations about God, Christian educators everywhere are eager to pass along the truth of our radically loving Savior to the next generation. And now we don't need to feel alone or under-equipped in that endeavor. David Staal has done all of us a great service by writing the book you hold in your hands. With wit and wisdom, his counsel will help us explain Scripture's life-giving message in language that little ones understand.

I'm hoping *Leading Kids to Jesus* will serve a wide audience. Because when parents and teachers are equipped to talk with youngsters, families will be strengthened, churches will move forward, and God will be pleased. A new generation of Christ-followers is on deck, ready to make its mark on the world. But first, these children need us to provide them with clear and age-appropriate explanations of God's timeless truth and limitless love.

Read this book and you'll be better prepared to lead and teach children. And then watch God do what he alone can accomplish: remake human hearts.

BILL HYBELS
Senior Pastor
Willow Creek Community Church

Acknowledgments

Becky—Thanks for your love, encouragement, ideas, and all the time you gave me to write.

Erin and Scott—Thanks for your love, cheers, and all you contributed to this book.

Judy Keene—Thanks for your friendship and for your expertise to ensure every word worked as it should. And for rewriting those that didn't.

Teri Lange—Thanks for the research and the support you give me throughout every day. It's a blast doing ministry with you.

Pat Cimo—Thanks for all the hours you spent reviewing drafts and for the great years of ministry together.

Sue Miller—Thanks for believing in me enough to choose me as a ministry partner, a friend, and an "e."

Bill Hybels—Thanks for building a church that offers opportunities for a guy like me to put my energy and talent to full use. (The jury's still out on the talent piece.)

Tammy Burke—Thanks for your support and constant reminders that I'm not crazy.

Paul Engle and Dawn Anderson—Thanks for your wisdom, edits, coaching, and confidence.

Starbucks team—The answer: 204 grandes or 25.5 gallons—roughly my entire body weight.

Promiseland programmers—Thanks for the creative assistance with wording.

Promiseland division leaders—Thanks for your help creating chapter 9.

Kristen Aikman—Thanks for your help crafting a conference session that has now grown up and become a book.

Garry Poole—Thanks for your deep friendship, ministry partnership, and for saying the words I needed to hear to start my walk with Christ.

Becky—Yes, you receive two acknowledgments because my love for you is greater than one acknowledgment could ever hold. I'm your man.

Introduction

O kay, I'll do it."

Those four small words combine to form a big statement because they transform one person's ideas into another person's actions. I said them to my close friend Garry Poole, Willow Creek Community Church's evangelism director, and immediately began to worry about the size of the commitment I had just made.

Our discussion had centered on the need for evangelism training in Promiseland, our children's ministry. Many adult ministries offered helpful instruction for their volunteers and staff, but Promiseland believed the materials they used did not connect strongly with its team. So Garry suggested that the coursework undergo modifications at the hand of one of his volunteers who had two kids, seemed to love children, and would likely say yes to this opportunity. I was that volunteer. Soon after Garry's call, I met with Pat Cimo, Promiseland's associate director, and several of her leaders to gather their input. This experience would soon validate my fear by proving that my commitment was indeed large. Very large.

During that meeting we discussed a major overhaul. The existing training was perfect for equipping adults to reach other adults with the good news about Jesus, but fell far short in helping with adult-child scenarios. And those situations occur frequently. At regular points throughout the ministry year, Promiseland's curriculum lessons include instructions for small group leaders to share their testimonies—the stories of how they became Christ-followers. This exercise always caused serious anxiety because leaders had to individually determine the right words to say and how to say them. In their struggle to do so, they might well have related to Mark Twain's well-known statement that "the difference between the right word and the almost right word is the difference between lightning and a lightning bug."[1]

With a full commissioning from the evangelism department and the children's ministry, I began a long journey to research and create a fresh training seminar. Once we offered these new materials to Promiseland small group leaders, the course continued to evolve with input from Pat and the ministry's executive director, Sue Miller. Eventually the course became a workshop taught at domestic and international Willow Creek Association Promiseland conferences. But I never imagined when I said, "Okay, I'll do it," that the journey would also include a book.

When I pictured spending time with you on the pages that follow, I realized that our conversation must favor inclusiveness. So the examples used, conclusions drawn, and skills described transcend denomination, Christian education program, or model of children's ministry. It was my hope that together, we'd travel down a road wide open to all Christ-followers who believe the common purpose that drives ministry to kids is simple: to help each one begin his or her life with Jesus.

Years of presenting this material to audiences large and small taught me the importance of people immediately putting the concepts discussed into practice. I knew that for this to happen in a book would require personal exercises after each chapter that enable you to fully engage what you've read.

To make the best use of your time, I also realized that this book must provide narrow focus. From cover to cover, it would be important for us to stay on a path concerned only with how to talk about God, Jesus, salvation, and other key spiritual topics in manners that make sense to a child. And our first step in that process would be to acknowledge that the right words play a big role.

Where do we find these words? The search to find child-appropriate terms and expressions reminds me of shopping for a left-handed baseball bat. A search through every sports store in town will never find one labeled for lefties. Any bat will work with either hand; the critical decision I face is to select the correct length and weight.

Your ministry effectiveness rests with your ability to select words well. Because when you step up to the plate and talk to a child about Jesus, a uniquely large Kingdom win might occur.

Dwight Moody understood the substantial victory that takes place when children accept Christ. After an outreach service at a local church, an acquaintance asked, "Reverend Moody, were there any converts tonight?"

The legendary evangelist said, "Yes, there were three and one-half."

The friend responded, "Ah, three adults and a child."

Moody clarified, "No, there were three children and an adult." He then continued, answering the bewildered look on the inquirer's face. "An adult only has half a life remaining to live for Christ, but the children will have the entirety of their lives to know His blessing and serve His will."[2]

I encourage you to prepare for salvation-centered discussions fueled by the joy of what could eventually happen—a child might say yes to Jesus, and an entire life might change. Realize, though, that this preparation requires effort. You might compare it to tuning, fueling, and loading up the family car with everything needed for the drive to a day at an amusement park—work that's easy to enjoy when you anticipate where you'll end up.

Amazingly, God trusts ordinary people like you and me with the divine privilege of helping lead kids into a life with Jesus. My wife and I know the thrill of that privilege firsthand, because our son and daughter have benefited from the very concepts and practices I now have the honor to share with you in these pages. That fact will keep me forever grateful that Garry chose me for an exciting Kingdom assignment.

And now I choose you.

CHAPTER 1

The Game Is One-on-One

S ome seek the thrill; others cringe in fear. The world consists of two types of people—those who like roller coasters and those who don't. I'm in the latter camp. So I felt a genuine jolt of panic when my son, Scott, met the minimum height requirement to ride a giant coaster during our annual trip to a nearby theme park.

The line for the premier attraction, one of the largest wooden roller coasters in the country, lasted ninety minutes. During this slow march to self-inflicted torture, I pictured every worst-case scenario we might encounter. Or so I thought. Finally, we stepped into the little car that would hurl us toward certain death. At least that's how I viewed it. Scott, on the other hand, jumped in and squirmed with excitement. As the iron safety bar lowered and locked across my lap, I grabbed it and told him, "Scotty, hold onto the bar like Daddy and do not let go!" My breathing was rapid and shallow, and veins on the top of my hands popped out as I clamped onto the bar of life.

The train of cars slowly ascended up the first hill, paused at the top, and then screamed down the track toward the ground. (Okay, it was not the car screaming, it was me!) Despite the growing gravitational force that invisibly pushed my head back, I managed to squeak out high-pitched words, "How ya doing, Scotty?"

"Not too good right now, Daddy," was the alarming response I heard.

Pure adrenalin washed away my fear when I saw what had happened. While the iron safety mechanism remained locked in place across my lap, a gap existed between Scott's much thinner lap and the bar. This resulted in my son slipping forward, barely on the seat at this point, with hands still clinging to the bar that was now at his neck.

Immediately I unglued my fingers from the bar and, in one big heave, pulled him upright and pressed the locking mechanism down farther. This meant the iron bar was now holding him securely but cutting off circulation to my lower body. I wisely reasoned, "Better to experience excruciating pain than to tell my wife I let our son fly off the roller coaster!"

I held onto him with one hand for the rest of the ride, while the other hand resumed its grip of life. As we climbed out of the car, I tried to control my trembling as Scott asked, "Can we go on it again?"

I share this story to illustrate an important point. Despite all the wonderful activities taking place throughout that theme park, and even surrounded by workers responsible for our safety and fun, I had to take appropriate action. And I had to do it alone. My response to my son made a big difference to him—possibly a life-or-death difference. Scott needed me.

In like fashion, crucial opportunities exist for anyone who spends time with kids. There will be times when you can make an eternal impact based on how you react—and someone will need you to do that well. Maybe you won't ever have to tighten a safety bar for a child, but you might play a role in locking in their salvation. And the purpose of this book is to prepare you to meet the challenge of those situations.

For sake of clarity, the focus of *Leading Kids to Jesus* is to equip adults to help kids start a life of faith by accepting Jesus as Lord and Savior. To that end, we'll examine how to do this as an individual—not through large outreach programs, elaborate presentations, or clever illustrations.

Specifically, preparation will focus on personal interactions —one-to-one conversations—with kids about key spiritual matters. This topic nearly bursts with importance because incredible and unpredictable opportunities for personal talks about faith exist both at church and at home. If you are a small group leader, Sunday school teacher, ministry director, Christian education worker, or children's church volunteer, this book is for you. Likewise, if you are a parent you'll find the concepts work well at home with your own kids, which is another reason this book is for you.

> There will be times when you can make an eternal impact based on how you react—and someone will need you to do that well.

And just as a ride on a coaster goes by fast, the time we have to impact youngsters also flies by quickly. So the time for preparation is now—because the urgency is real.

SALVATION AT AN EARLY AGE

Respected pollster George Barna conducted studies to determine the probability that people of various ages will ask Jesus to be their Savior. The results heavily favor children five through twelve years old:

Probability of Asking Jesus to Be Savior

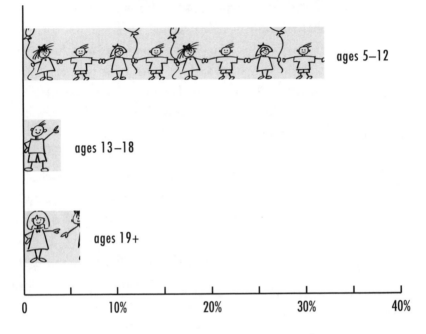

ages 5–12

ages 13–18

ages 19+

| 0 | 10% | 20% | 30% | 40% |

Barna's conclusion? "If people do not embrace Jesus Christ as their Savior before they reach their teenage years, their chance of doing so at all is slim."[1]

Author and speaker Karyn Henley agrees that kids are more inclined than adults to accept the gospel. She writes, "Children are more likely to express a matter-of-fact faith in God than we adults who only believe in what we can experience with our five senses."[2]

The Bible dispels any skepticism about the validity of a kid's matter-of-fact faith. Just look at Acts 2:39 in which Peter says, "The promise is for you and your *children* and for all who are far off—for all whom the Lord our God will call" (emphasis added). The Greek word used in this verse (*teknon*) literally means "child"—as in a daughter or son.[3] The promise Peter speaks of is that of salvation, and clearly it's available to kids. Romans 10:9 reveals the criteria for salvation: "If you confess with your mouth, 'Jesus is Lord,' and believe in your heart that

God raised him from the dead, you will be saved." This verse articulates the inclusive nature of God's saving grace and mandates no minimum age.

Of course the ability to comprehend the promise and the timing in which it happens varies by person—whether child or adult. Focus on the Family's Dr. James Dobson describes his salvation experience at age three.[4] Moody Bible Institute's former president, Joe Stowell, accepted Christ at six.[5] Evangelist Billy Graham made his decision at sixteen.[6] Although I hesitate to mention my name in the same paragraph with the previous three, I gave my life to Jesus at age twenty-nine (although still a kid at heart).

> So armed with assurance from Scripture that kids can enter an authentic relationship with the Lord, the question becomes *how*?

So armed with assurance from Scripture that kids *can* enter an authentic relationship with the Lord, along with numerous examples that children *do* commit their young lives to Jesus, the question becomes *how*?

A PERSONAL APPROACH

Many children's ministries answer that question with clear and relevant lessons, accompanied by creative Bible teaching. Incredible salvation messages for kids have become plentiful and readily available, and certainly enjoy success. But they represent only one approach. Because when one of these programs or lessons ends, little eyes frequently scan for adults in the room while their little minds formulate big questions.

What happens next contributes mightily to a ministry's ability to reach its full impact. The adults in that room can help individual kids cross the line of salvation by engaging in simple conversations. Oftentimes, the situation calls for clear, plain talk about a relationship with Jesus. Or maybe answers to questions about God and heaven. These simple exchanges at church (or home) can have profound effects—but they call for preparation, because the stakes are high.

When Dennis was a young boy, he expressed a desire to start a relationship with Jesus. So his mother took him to meet with a staff member at their church. This person explained several biblical concepts and prayed the salvation prayer for Dennis. It wasn't until many years later that Dennis, in a conversation with his small group leader, heard about the need to pray for himself. Now he wishes he had learned that critical piece of the process earlier in life.

Sure, when my son or daughter expresses interest in hearing about how someone gets to heaven, I could schedule a meeting with a staff member at my church and let the "professional" do the talking. No one would call me a bad parent. Or as a kids' small group leader, when one of the boys in my group asks me what it means to be a Christian, I could find one of the large group teachers or the ministry director to offer an explanation. But do either of those approaches fully serve the child involved?

Deferring to someone more qualified or experienced feels more comfortable, because I avoid an encounter with my own fearful thought, What if I don't say the right thing? But consider the child's viewpoint. If the adult she is close to hesitates to talk about Jesus on a personal level, will Jesus seem close by or far off? Even if the reason for the handoff stems from the adult's uncertainty about how to say what he knows in a kid-friendly way, the impact is equally confusing.

Conversely, imagine the potential impact on a child who listens to his parent's from-the-heart story of faith. Or the potential unleashed when an adult at Sunday school offers a simple clarification of what it means to be a Christian, answering a question the child didn't want to ask in front of everyone. It's easy to believe that a child in either situation might be encouraged to start a relationship with Jesus right then and there.

Your Role

Now imagine *you* are that parent or that children's ministry worker. Sometimes you will enter moments with kids when their eternal destinies are as close as the air you breathe, if you can simply speak the right words. In their language. Because the terms and analogies mature Christians use to discuss faith issues with each other are likely to be lost on kids.

Ron, a children's ministry volunteer, had the spontaneous opportunity one weekend to share his testimony with a boy in his group who asked if Ron was a Christian. After two minutes of confusing language peppered with plenty of "ums" and "uhs," the conversation went elsewhere. Opportunity lost.

This scenario is easy to remedy—simply prepare to say the right words whenever the right opportunity arrives. Scripture points out that deliberate attention to language will benefit both the recipient ("A word aptly spoken is like apples of gold in settings of silver," Proverbs 25:11) and the speaker ("A man finds joy in giving an apt reply," Proverbs 15:23).

But don't let those Bible verses take you to the conclusion that what's needed is for adults to hand kids a heavy load of theology. Yes, fluency with Paul's conversion on the Damascus road serves as a useful reminder of how Jesus changes lives. Even more valuable, though, is the confidence to describe the path you took to become a Christ-follower—or how the child you're talking with can walk the same steps. Eager willingness to engage in the latter could change the world of a young one—and you'll need to hold onto a safety bar to handle your excitement!

Even if you feel fairly confident in your ability to have such conversations, commit to polish your skills further. You'll celebrate your readiness when a child needs you.

A Willow Creek sermon series titled "Just Walk Across the Room" focused on developing a willingness to be used by the Holy Spirit for spiritual conversations with others not yet in God's family. "I enjoy [doing] many things in life," said senior pastor Bill Hybels. "But I don't know if there's anything I like better than that moment when someone says, 'I'll be grateful for all eternity for what you did when you walked across that room....' That's as good as it gets."[7] Confidently engaging people provides exhilarating benefits.

The payoff—the thrill—Bill de-scribes is real. Double the thrill if that conversation is with a youngster trusted to your care as part of a small group or Sunday school class. And triple the thrill if the child is your son or daughter.

So if you work with kids at church, determine now to become even more prepared for unscripted, unplanned scenes when you talk with a child about faith—his or hers and your own. No workbooks, no notes, no kidding. Or if you're a parent, commit to becoming fluent with simple personal faith explanations so that you're ready for any bedtime conversation that may become a real-time salvation opportunity. Even if you feel fairly confident in your ability to have such conversations, commit to polish your skills further. You'll celebrate your readiness when a child needs you.

Such a need materialized for Beth, a ministry team colleague, while in the family car on an errand.

> One day while in the car, my four-year-old daughter asked what would happen if I died. I was caught a little off guard since we went from talking about the weather to dying in the same brief exchange.
>
> Maty, very distressed, said, "Mom, I don't want you to die."
>
> I tried to comfort her. "Maty," I said, "you know I made a decision a long time ago to ask Jesus to be my forever friend. The Bible says if you love God and Jesus then you can go to heaven when you die. So you see, I'm not afraid of dying because I know that I'm going to heaven."
>
> For the next couple of moments, I really felt like time had stopped. "Mom!" she said, with much excitement, "I love God and Jesus!"
>
> "Well," I said, "have you ever asked him to forgive you and be your forever friend?"
>
> She quietly said, "No."

I couldn't believe how God had prepared me to ask the next question. I had participated in some training at church a few times that readied me for exactly what to say next.

I continued to navigate through traffic, and with my hands gripped tightly on the steering wheel, I said, "Would you like to pray right now?"

She answered, "Yes." As we began to pray the salvation prayer, I was overwhelmed with gratitude. My own daughter was the first person I have ever had the privilege of praying the prayer with. I will be glad forever that I was prepared for that conversation—God used me!

Beth knew the right words to say, but it's a safe bet that many of us would have succumbed to a variety of self-doubts. What if I say something wrong? What if I'm asked a tough question? Do I know enough about the Bible? Can I put my faith into words? Finding the right words can be a challenge. But that need not be the case.

Booker T. Washington once shared a story about a ship lost at sea for many days that sighted a friendly vessel. The crew of the unfortunate vessel signaled, "Water, water: we die of thirst!" An immediate answer from the friendly vessel came back: "Cast down your buckets where you are." They answered a second, third, and fourth signal for water: "Cast down your buckets where you are." The captain of the distressed vessel finally heeded the advice, and the buckets came up full of fresh, sparkling water from the mouth of the Amazon River.[8]

The thirsty crew in Mr. Washington's story learned that the solution to their challenge lay close at hand and within their ability to grasp. Similarly, I'm confident that finding the right words to share with kids will be as easy for you as finding water proved to be for those sailors. And toward that end, this book provides practical guidance on what to say, tips on how to say it, and even ways for you to communicate in profound ways without saying a thing. The best part is that you can accomplish all this without radical changes to your ministry or enrolling in theology classes. If you have regular proximity to kids in church or at home, opportunities for important one-on-one spiritual conversations will likely present themselves more often than you think.

This simple, personal adventure of preparation will change your perspective about how evangelism to kids takes place. Consider for a moment the deep difference between asking God to use *your ministry* to reach kids for Jesus and asking God to equip and use *you personally* to reach children for him. For parents, it's the difference between the prayers, "God, please help my child know you," and "God, please use me to help my kid start a relationship with you."

So if life seems like a roller coaster with the kids close at hand, or even if you're still waiting in line for that excitement, together we'll find the words kids need to hear. Hold on tight and keep turning the pages. In fact, when you turn this one, you'll head back to the theme park to learn the basic principles of effective communication with kids. Get ready for what could be the ride of your life!

Personal Exercises

1. Rate your confidence level in talking with individual children about salvation.

    1   2   3   4   5   6   7   8   9   10

    low, avoid at all costs   high, I could write a book

2. Rate how frequently you engage in personal spiritual conversations with kids.

    1   2   3   4   5   6   7   8   9   10

    never, even if I'm cornered   always, every time I'm near a child

3. Rate the effectiveness of these conversations.

    1   2   3   4   5   6   7   8   9   10

    ineffective, kids leave me thoroughly confused   highly effective, kids leave me thoroughly saved

4. How do your responses to the first three questions relate to each other?

5. What would you like your scores to be after reading this book?

CHAPTER 2

Communicating with Kids

The weather forecast called for a hot, sticky day — and the weatherman's prediction was right on the mark. Although late July in the Midwest is a great time to swim in a pool, it is far short of an ideal time to walk through a crowded theme park. But there we were, my five-year-old son Scott and I, constantly seeking shade and drinking our weight in lemonade. Unfortunately, the fun was melting faster than the ice in our cups.

My spirits lifted when I spotted the Logger's Run. Simpler than most of the attractions, this ride featured a lazy float in a loglike boat along a river channel that led to a waterfall's brim. Then came a sudden long drop that bottomed out in a big wet splash, appearing to bring refreshment well worth a second or two of terror. "Hey Scott," I said, "want to go on this ride so we can cool off?"

"Sure," he replied.

Even the hour-plus wait in line took place in the shade, so it looked like smooth sailing to me. Finally our turn came to step into a log, and Scott and I took the front two spots out of the log's four. I noticed no iron restraining bars, so concluded the drop must not be dangerous. Two teenage girls boarded the back seats, and our voyage began.

We meandered through the channel for a few minutes, then paused momentarily before the big plunge. Even though most logs skimmed the water surface at the bottom of the fall, ours didn't. Because Scott and I were in the first two seats, the log was very front heavy. Okay, to be fair to him, the weight imbalance was due to me. Regardless of the reason, the nose of our log dove into the water like a duck bobbing for food—and took all of us down with it. While most people got showered from the big splash, those aboard our log took a bath. We didn't sink in over our heads, but we definitely experienced 100 percent saturation from mid-torso down. And I loved it!

But I sat alone in my joy. The quiet ride to the disembark ramp hinted that a problem existed. The two girls and I quickly exited the log. Then, as I offered Scott a steady hand to step out, I asked him if he liked it. His response confirmed we had a problem. He burst into tears.

"What's wrong, buddy?" I asked.

"You didn't say we'd get wet!" he yelled back.

"Wait a minute," I reasoned, "what did you think I meant when I said we'd cool off?"

He paused to catch his breath and then blurted out, "I thought it was going to be air-conditioned!"

WHAT'S SAID VS. WHAT'S UNDERSTOOD

I'll never forget the lesson I learned as we stood there dripping in front of a crowd now staring at us—unless I'm careful, I can do a real poor job of using words that children fully understand.

This is a common challenge for adults. Especially Christian ones. Listen closely as some of them speak about spiritual life, and you may hear a language all its own. It might require years to learn—and that poses a problem. Christianity has the greatest message in the world, but it won't have any impact when delivered with descriptions that come close to being in code to those outside the circle.

This disconnect is even more obvious when it involves children. Sure, it creates humorous moments for parents to chuckle over or even write about in a book someday. But it also frequently, and unintentionally, stands in the way of meaningful dialogue about spiritual issues. Which is no laughing matter.

> Christianity has the greatest message in the world, but it won't have any impact when delivered with descriptions that come close to being in code to those outside the circle.

In *The Gentle Art of Communicating with Kids*, Dr. Suzette Elgin underscores this issue when she says, "The only meaning a sequence of language has is the meaning the listener understands it to have."[1] Consider the implications of her statement. It doesn't matter what you say; what matters is how a child *interprets* what you say. On the same track, basketball Hall of Fame coach Red Auerbach offered a tip to coaches that lends itself to our topic: "It's not what you tell your players that counts; it's what they hear."[2]

This chapter was designed to help you close the gap between what you say and what children understand you to have just said. The remainder of the book will build off the foundation laid by the following four key dynamics of communication with kids.

Dynamic 1—Children understand concrete terms and language better than they understand abstract terms and language. In other words, children are likely to be much more literal than adults. The adult application of this dynamic is easy—avoid symbolism or "religious" words. A few examples of what to steer clear of may help.

"Ask Jesus into your heart" is a common confusion-causer. Sure, some kids understand this statement, but many don't. Although a child might not say so, she may wonder how Jesus can physically fit into such a small space. A place inside her kid-sized body, no less! What the adult who says, "Ask Jesus into your heart," really means is "Start a personal relationship with Christ today."

"Pay the price for your sins" is another phrase to reconsider. A young boy in our children's ministry program once told me he would try to save up his allowance to cover the payment himself! Although we didn't discuss the actual amount he receives, it took him quite a while to understand that he could never save enough. And that money was not the real issue.

> Our challenge, then, is to avoid the use of analogy, symbolism, or any abstract wording that requires familiarity with a concept.

Our challenge, then, is to avoid the use of analogy, symbolism, or any abstract wording that requires familiarity with a concept. Likewise, we must take care to maintain our intended meaning when we select concrete terms. (Alternative wording to common Christian words appears in chapter 4, which focuses on explaining the gospel message.)

A tempting shortcut to eliminate abstract language is merely to avoid difficult words. That, however, isn't always the solution. Common sense says we should not use long, complicated terms. "Substitutionary atoning sacrifice" contains three weighty words that most people wouldn't dream of saying to a six-year-old. (And probably not even to one another!) But the simpler phrase "perfect lamb who carried my sins" can just as easily lead toward confusion. Why would a baby sheep carry sins? Even relatively simple words can combine to form complex phrases or analogies that encrypt the meaning from children, who naturally assign literal meaning to words.

Jesus' disciples provide an excellent example of the confusion literal meaning can generate. In Matthew 16:6, Jesus warns them, "Be on your guard against the yeast of the Pharisees and Sadducees." Even though the disciples heard him speak in parables on other occasions, they jumped to a literal translation of Jesus' imagery. They assumed he was referring to their failure to pack bread for their journey. With a touch of exasperation, he explains what he meant. "Then they understood that he was not telling them to guard against the yeast used in bread, but against the teaching of the Pharisees and Sadducees" (verse 12).

Today's children should not be expected to understand more than Christ's disciples! The answer to the dilemma of abstract wording is to use concrete, or literal, terms. Clarity requires that we use the words kids need to hear, which likely differ from the words adults typically speak to one another. Although there's nothing technically wrong with "laying my sins at the foot of the cross," the words "telling God I'm sorry for the wrong things I've done" conveys the same message in a way a child can far more easily understand.

The need for sensitivity to the issue of abstract language decreases as children's ages increase, but so does their likelihood of becoming Christ-followers. As I mentioned earlier, pollster George Barna's research shows that children are most likely to become Christians before age thirteen. As a person who beat the odds and gave my life to Christ as an adult, I know that at any age, people outside the family of God will benefit from concrete language in discussions about faith. In 1 Corinthians 2:1, Paul provides an excellent model to follow: "When I came to you, brothers and sisters, I did not come proclaiming the mystery of God to you in lofty words or wisdom" (NRSV).

Dynamic 2—Children are at different developmental levels. Age affects a child's ability to understand, no matter how simply you word the concepts you want to communicate. A child's age will partner with such factors as education, family and social surroundings, and life experiences to influence his or her intellect and spiritual knowledge. These factors will make a difference in how we communicate with kids.

For example, my ten-year-old son works on long multiplication problems, while my seven-year-old daughter labors with double-digit addition. Neither is better than the other, they're just at different levels. In a one-to-one conversation, a child's age will dictate how simple I need to deliberately stay with the language I speak and the concepts I explain. Recently I learned yet again that age isn't the only factor.

I coach my son's park district league basketball team. This season, a first-year player named Matthew joined our team of

eight veterans. He's a great kid with a smile as big as the court we play on. During a scrimmage, I gave Matthew a specific assignment. "When the other team makes a basket," I said, "then you take the ball out of bounds."

"Okay, Coach," he replied with his signature grin.

Everyone on the team understood my instructions meant that after opponents score, Matthew should grab the ball, step behind the black line under the basket, and then throw the ball to a teammate. Everyone, that is, except Matthew.

Moments later, a player on the other team sunk a basket that set up Matthew's big role. Confidently, he grabbed the ball and stood behind the out-of-bounds line. And stood there. I whistled for play to stop, and asked Matthew why he wasn't throwing the ball. The smile disappeared. I ran over to him, where he quietly informed me that I told him to take the ball out of bounds; I did not say to throw it to anyone.

He was right, and I was wrong. I did not consider Matthew's level of experience when I explained his assignment. I assumed that he would know what I meant. That moment caused me to start coaching to fit each player. We resumed practice with a wiser coach. Fortunately, Matthew's smile resumed as well.

The application to all of us who serve as small group leaders or Sunday school teachers is clear—even in the same age-group or class, kids may occupy very different levels of understanding. So leaders and teachers must make certain that their word choices fit each child. Putting this concept into practice means constantly self-checking my assumptions. Often the remedy is simple—such as adding the words "and throw it to someone on your team" to my basketball instructions. Other times a lack of knowledge is not the issue. Perhaps plenty of learning has taken place, which may or may not be a good thing.

Some children come to church having heard wonderful things at home about God and Jesus. Other kids arrive knowing different names of God only as the beginnings of curses. This difference can become a big factor if the gospel is explained using an assumption of reverence for the Almighty. In addition, while one child will have warm, loving feelings when he hears about "God the Father," another will wince at the thought of dad because of a troubled home life. Maybe this child's father has permanently left home, or is a source of pain when he's present. Could this be why the child doesn't seem interested in having a relationship with God? Although the reasons vary, kids of similar age and appearance can be at dramatically different spiritual developmental levels.

> Even in the same age-group or class, kids may occupy very different levels of understanding.

So while conversing with kids, don't hesitate to call a time-out to check whether they understand what you're saying. Consider any assumptions you might be making. And always be willing to adapt your words to suit them. The more you tailor comments to what you know about a child's developmental level, the better you can serve him or her.

Dynamic 3 — Children are most receptive to stories and terms they can relate to or picture. While growing up, I loved to watch the Peanuts television specials. As an adult, I still enjoy them. The story lines, characters, and timeless humor combine to serve as proof of Charles Schultz's genius. My favorite scenes among his numerous made-for-television shows were those times a kid sat in class listening to the teacher talk. The teacher, never shown, always said the same thing: "Wah, wah, wah, waaaah." Just the memory of that sound makes me chuckle as I write this paragraph.

Adults often quote the Peanuts teacher and her highly memorable lines. "Wah, wah, wah, waaaah" communicates jesting mockery of someone's longer-than-necessary droning on a subject, or delivery of a boring lecture. I remember, as a youngster, saying it once as I rolled my eyes in response to something my dad told me. Never tried it again.

The point is that no one, especially a child, enjoys a lecture. In fact, kids will understand far more of what an adult attempts to explain when that adult uses a brief story. Children love stories! Especially short ones. Kids will also engage with what's said at a deeper level when a leader or teacher uses words that refer to something familiar to them—creating a connection between the story and the listener. Let's look at a practical example.

In chapter 1, I described my friend Dennis's journey to Jesus. When he shares it with second- or third-grade boys in our children's ministry, he starts by saying, "Guys, I'd like to tell you a story about a young guy your age who liked to play baseball, soccer, and basketball. He wasn't always the best kid on the team, and didn't always get picked first to play." For the next minute or two, saucer-sized eyes follow Dennis and his every word.

One reason Dennis is so effective at sharing his testimony is his ability to draw kids in—they want to hear what he has to say. He tells them a story rather than lecturing. He seasons that story with points that are familiar to second- and third-grade boys. If a boy likes sports, he'll relate to Dennis's tale. If he doesn't like sports, he'll relate to how the boy in the story didn't get picked first to play.

Jesus often used story-based teaching. He told the tale of the good Samaritan (Luke 10) in response to a question that he could easily have answered with a fact or lecture on who to consider as a neighbor. Instead, he chose to share a story that illustrated the concept of "neighbor" to all who listened.

We too can use this technique, which is sometimes referred to as painting a word picture. If I include one or more parallels with a youngster's life in what I say, that child pictures a scenario and interest rapidly rises. Finding a commonality to mention is often as easy as making reference to a generic part of kids' lives. For instance, "You know how you have many choices about what to play during recess ..." or some similar statement will let kids know that this story is going to apply to them.

Another way to engage a child in a story is through well-timed questions that spark thoughts but don't require extended pondering. Have you ever observed someone do this particularly well? That question invites your brief mental participation as a reader, but doesn't go down a long tangent. "Have you ever thought about that?" "Can you imagine how she felt?" "You've never done that, have you?" Examples of such questions in conversation could go on for pages.

These questions don't require long responses, if any at all. Use them, instead, to provoke thought. They involve the listener. They allow you to talk *with* a child rather than *at* her. And they keep you from sounding like the Peanuts teacher.

There is, however, a big qualifier to consider. Keep reading.

Dynamic 4—Children may focus on, or be distracted by, a single detail in a story. Like many people, my life's been full of ups and downs, bumps and bruises, and plenty of valuable lessons. A generous amount of that learning occurred while I worked in the National Football League. But if I start to tell another person about any life issue I tackled during my brief stint with the Indianapolis Colts, the conversation typically takes an abrupt turn. The person I'm talking with attempts to picture me in full pads and a helmet and usually takes a guess at what position I played. The disappointment lasts only momentarily when I reveal that I worked in the public relations department!

Now imagine if I were to mention this life experience while sharing my personal testimony with an elementary school–aged boy. He might get excited to hear about an interview I conducted with Bears running back Walter Payton, but then I'll have to struggle to get the conversation back to the original spiritual topic. So I've learned to carefully consider details I share in a story with kids.

Consider the impact of sharing a story with a child that describes how Jesus can help a person conquer alcohol or drug abuse. Of course Christ can prove victorious in such a situation; that's not the issue. An issue arises if a child listening to this story is on the receiving end of the results of substance abuse at home. If that's the case, the victimized kid is likely to place the redeemed adult in the category of very bad people.

Susan Shadid, Promiseland's training director, offers a valuable perspective on considering details as they relate to a much more common conversation topic. She specifically advises adults not to dwell too heavily on heaven alone as the reason for salvation. "Spending eternity with God in heaven is a cornerstone of becoming a Christian that kids need to understand," she says. "But if that's the exclusive focus, some kids—especially younger ones—could become scared of Christianity because they might believe people who accept Christ have to die soon after."

> Reexamine our details and be sensitive to their impact on our listeners.

Don't misinterpret this dynamic. It doesn't advise us to refrain from storytelling or to leave out key spiritual truths. The counsel is to reexamine our details and to be sensitive to their impact on our listeners. Often, rewording is all that's needed to maintain meaning without introducing distractions. On a lighter note, if my story were to include anything about drinking water, I might have a kid in the small group I lead suddenly become desperate for a trip to a water fountain—a desperation sure to be contagious with the other kids. My only hope at that point would be to ask if anyone might want to hear about my professional football days!

STARTING POINTS

If you believe the challenge of successfully applying these four dynamics every time you chat with kids seems large, then you are thinking realistically. Success will come with practice. And that's okay. I've taught these dynamics for several years, but still have to throw the penalty flag on myself every now and then. A realistic and wise starting point is to actively listen to the descriptive language kids use in your locale. If you work in children's ministry, listen closely while kids interact with one another in church and nonchurch settings. If you're a parent, pay attention to conversations your children have with others.

Take a few moments to picture life from a kid's perspective before you have an opportunity for a faith discussion. Envision right now what you might say about the basics of Christianity. What do you think would make sense to a child? What do you have in common with the kids you are around? What connections exist between the unique life they experience and truths in the Bible? (Hint: the list is quite long.) The challenge here is for you to give thought to what you might say, applying the four dynamics, *before* you have to say it.

For more specific preparation, ask a kid to describe his or her relationship with Jesus for you, and tune in closely to the words you hear. If you're not in a position to make this request easily and naturally with a child you know well, then I will lend you my daughter's assistance. When she was seven years old, she wrote her thoughts about being in a relationship with Jesus as if she were telling a friend. I call it the Gospel According to Erin. Here's what she wrote (with plenty of help from our computer's auto spelling/grammar function):

> You have to know Jesus before you do it [pray]. You have to know that he came down to earth for us. He explained to people how to live and treat people nice. So that we could go to heaven, he died on a cross. It's like people know him here, but he's really in heaven, but not dead. Jesus cleans us of the wrong things we've done just like taking a bath with soap.
>
> This is how to be a forever friend with Jesus! Just pray — "In my life, I have done a lot of stuff wrong and I want to go to heaven. So I want what Jesus did when he died to count for me. Please be with me all my life, and help me live my life like you want me to. Amen!"
>
> But you can only be somebody's best friend if you meet them, and that's how you need to be with Jesus — you need to meet him and get to know him and then say that prayer.
>
> The coolest part of being Jesus' forever friend is that he is always with you! Sometimes I say, "Jesus, I'm scared, help me." Then sometimes he makes me not scared. But when he doesn't, I just run into Mom and Dad's room.
>
> I wish everyone could be Jesus' friend.

Erin uses simpler words than you and I might normally select. Yet her language still communicates the message of Christ, and would likely prove effective with young listeners. Adopting a manner that focuses on the listener is a worthy challenge, but not a new concept.

In Acts 2, on the day of Pentecost when the Holy Spirit descended upon the believers, the wind howled and what looked like tongues of fire touched all who were there. What happened next relates to our challenge. The people outside of the building in which all of this happened heard individuals speaking in their native languages—and the multicultured words seemed to come from the homogenous group of Christ-followers. The reaction was one of astonishment; "We hear them declaring the wonders of God in our own tongues! . . . What does this mean?" (verses 11, 12).

For us, it means that when we keep in mind the four key dynamics of communicating with kids, then we will declare the wonders of God in ways that they will understand—no tongues of fire required! These principles will increase the effectiveness of conversations with children regardless of the topic. Besides, kids think it's cool when an adult explains something to them in a way that they truly understand.

So let's put the four key dynamics to work. The next chapter walks through step-by-step training to prepare any adult to share his or her own story about becoming a Christian. After that, we'll look at explaining the plan of salvation, then how to pray to become a Christ-follower.

Personal Exercises

1. Write abstract terms and language you've heard used in children's ministry that likely confuse kids. Have you ever said any of them?

2. List the names of children that you regularly interact with in ministry. Beside each name, write one or more items that impact the child's developmental level.

3. Develop a list of bullet points that describes kids' lives today. In addition to culture and activities, include typical attitudes toward God, Jesus, church, and Christianity. Underline items similar to your childhood years. Keep this list as a guide for relating to kids.

CHAPTER 3

Share Your Story

The honor of being the best-known theme park belongs to Disney World in Orlando, Florida. A visit to Disney thrills virtually any child. In fact, merely the anticipation of the trip generates fun. At least it did for my wife and me, which prompted us to announce to our kids, "We're going to Disney World!" a full year prior to our trip. We intended to squeeze as much excitement as possible out of the entire experience—and that included the planning process.

So while I spent months whooping up excitement at home, my wife practically earned an advanced degree in Disney trip planning. Phone calls, conversations with other families, books, Web searches—she did it all. And when we arrived, we followed her detailed plan to make the most of every moment. My job was to carry the luggage. With a smile.

The result of Becky's tireless research was a trip that maximized its potential for joy because we knew the hot spots, cool rides, and strategies to avoid long lines. Although several books claim to give you great tips about Disney, we found that the stories and recommendations from people we know always proved to be golden advice.

This was especially true for our daughter, Erin. Her best friend Lauren repeatedly told her that the coolest ride at Disney is Space Mountain—an enormous indoor roller coaster that shoots you through space. Unfortunately for me, in addition to luggage duty I'm also the designated rider. Based on Lauren's enthusiastic endorsement of Space Mountain, Erin's mind was made up that we would spend every spare moment tossed to the outer reaches of the galaxy. At least my son prefers roller coasters located in daylight, where I can see what drop or turn approaches (when my eyes are open, that is).

To be fair, other Disney attractions also offer worthy challenges to someone like me. In hindsight, I'm not sure which experience gripped me most intensely—the feeling that my life would end on Space Mountain or wishing it would end on the boat ride that featured thousands of dolls chanting, "It's a small world after all." Fortunately, the latter did not make Lauren's recommendation list, so it had no chance of making the "let's go on it again" roster we kept. But Space Mountain did.

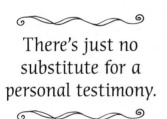

There's just no substitute for a personal testimony.

After our third turn battling death–by–roller coaster in near darkness, I understood the high value kids place on other people's experiences. Without her friend's personal testament and encouragement, my daughter and I would have braved other adventures. But we trusted her buddy because friends can be trusted to tell the truth—much more so than any messages, signs, or persuasion offered by other attractions. There's just no substitute for a personal testimony.

As much fun as Space Mountain is (if you're Erin or Lauren), the thrill pales in comparison to the most incredible ride in life—a relationship with Jesus. Just ask any Christ-follower to share his or her personal testimony. Or should you? Just because a person has a testimony doesn't guarantee an ability to share it well. Fortunately, a reasonable dose of preparation is all that's needed to sharply increase the odds that it will be effective.

THE BASICS OF A STRONG TESTIMONY

The very best way to begin that preparation is to consider the story of how you became a Christian. Why that story? Because a personal testimony carries considerable weight. It offers real value to the listener. When you share your journey to faith, you illustrate that Jesus changes real people's lives today, not just the lives of folks in the Bible two thousand years ago. A testimony makes the vast concepts of Christianity intensely personal and believable.

Consider this analogy: a conversation about football with buddies around the watercooler is very different from a conversation about football with an NFL player. Why? Because with the player, you can discuss actual game experience with someone who really plays the sport, not one who simply watches and talks about it. And although many people have observations and opinions about religion, you might be the only adult Christian that some people know. You might be the only one they can trust—the only one in the game and willing to tackle a topic like a personal faith experience.

Willow Creek's senior pastor Bill Hybels affirms the value of such a conversation, "The greatest gift you can give someone is the story of Jesus and how He changes lives—especially yours."[1] This gift needs thoughtful wrapping, though, to make it effective. To that end, Bill lists key attributes worthy of careful attention:[2]

> Make it clear.
> Use the right terminology.
> Keep it short.

Left unattended, my story would run counter to these guidelines. Maybe yours would too. Add to this list a requirement
to relate well to kids, and the need
for work becomes obvious. The rest
of this chapter will help us craft and
polish our personal stories, enabling
us to confidently and effectively
share them with children.

> Think of your
> testimony
> as what follows the
> lead-in statement,
> "Here's what
> happened to me."

Fortunately, receptivity to the
"greatest gift you can give someone"
will be high, especially in kids. Illinois state Teacher of the Year award
winner Bob Grimm articulates this
point when he counsels educators, "Tell kids stories about yourself; they want to hear them."[3]

Think of your testimony as what follows the lead-in statement, "Here's what happened to me." And accept the responsibility to communicate that story well. This is a worthy
challenge when you consider the potential outcome: I can help
kids understand *their* need for personal relationships with Jesus
when I share with them about *my* personal relationship with
Jesus. You can too. So let's build our stories.

COACHING FROM AN APOSTLE

We'll base our testimonies on a three-part outline designed to
serve as a memory tool and an organizational aid. To deliver
your story, you must be able to quickly remember it. And
to deliver your story well requires that you articulate it with
logic that other people can easily follow. Mark Mittelberg, Bill
Hybels, and Lee Strobel, authors of the *Becoming a Contagious
Christian* training course, suggest that we follow the direction
found in Acts 26 and examine the three-part approach used
by Paul.

His testimony contains three very distinct, sequential periods of time. While we look at Paul's words, consider your own story and life experiences, and specifically how you would describe your life using these three eras: before becoming a Christian (call it "BC"), your conversion ("the Cross"), and life after becoming a Christian ("AD"). Questions along the way will prompt you through this self-reflection process; your answers will serve as building blocks later in the chapter.

BC (before becoming a Christian)

Paul begins his personal testimony to King Agrippa with a description of life before becoming a Christ-follower:

> The Jews all know the way I have lived ever since I was a child, from the beginning of my life in my own country, and also in Jerusalem. They have known me for a long time and can testify, if they are willing, that according to the strictest sect of our religion, I lived as a Pharisee. And now it is because of my hope in what God has promised our fathers that I am on trial today. This is the promise our twelve tribes are hoping to see fulfilled as they earnestly serve God day and night. O king, it is because of this hope that the Jews are accusing me. Why should any of you consider it incredible that God raises the dead?
>
> I too was convinced that I ought to do all that was possible to oppose the name of Jesus of Nazareth. And that is just what I did in Jerusalem. On the authority of the chief priests I put many of the saints in prison, and when they were put to death, I cast my vote against them. Many a time I went from one synagogue to another to have them punished, and I tried to force them to blaspheme. In my obsession against them, I even went to foreign cities to persecute them.
>
> (Acts 26:4–11)

Paul uses very specific language that paints a vivid picture of him as a zealous Pharisee and staunch oppressor of Jesus' followers. The importance of such descriptors is that they set up the life change that Jesus brings. Everyone has had life experience before they met Jesus as Lord and Savior. Most were not as vicious as Paul's, yet all of us were equally lost. Because this era is before Christ, it's referred to as BC.

To help stimulate ideas for your BC era, write key words that come to mind when considering these two questions:

1. What were you like, personally and/or spiritually, before becoming a Christ-follower?
2. What caused you to begin considering a move toward God/Christ?

The Cross (conversion)

In Acts 26:12–18, Paul provides details of his conversion along the Damascus road:

On one of these journeys I was going to Damascus with the authority and commission of the chief priests. About noon, O king, as I was on the road, I saw a light from heaven, brighter than the sun, blazing around me and my companions. We all fell to the ground, and I heard a voice saying to me in Aramaic, "Saul, Saul, why do you persecute me? It is hard for you to kick against the goads."

Then I asked, "Who are you, Lord?"

"I am Jesus, whom you are persecuting," the Lord replied. "Now get up and stand on your feet. I have appeared to you to appoint you as a servant and as a witness of what you have seen of me and what I will show you. I will rescue you from your own people and from the Gentiles. I am sending you to them to open their eyes and turn them from darkness to light, and from the power of Satan to God, so that they may receive forgiveness of sins and a place among those who are sanctified by faith in me."

In these verses, Paul clearly recounts how he met Jesus, and he does so in a manner easy to understand. Notice that the description remains tightly focused on Paul's experience and does not expand into a lecture on the salvation plan. Because this era is the point Christ enters Paul's life and converts him, it's called "the Cross."

To help stimulate ideas for your Cross era, write key words that come to mind when considering these two questions:

1. What realization did you come to that finally motivated you to follow Christ?
2. Specifically, what did you do to become a Christian?

AD (after becoming a Christian)

The third part of the story in Acts 26 features Paul's life after his conversion:

> So then, King Agrippa, I was not disobedient to the vision from heaven. First to those in Damascus, then to those in Jerusalem and in all Judea, and to the Gentiles also, I preached that they should repent and turn to God and prove their repentance by their deeds. That is why the Jews seized me in the temple courts and tried to kill me. But I have had God's help to this very day, and so I stand here and testify to small and great alike.
>
> (verses 19–22)

Deep contrast exists between the Paul in verses 19–22 and the man described in 4–11. And therein lies the power of a personal testimony—a life clearly changed as a result of Jesus. Because Paul describes the different man he became after Jesus entered the picture, this era is known as AD.

To help stimulate ideas for the AD era, write key words that come to mind when considering these two questions:

1. How did your life begin to change after you began to follow Christ?
2. What are clear differences in your life now that you follow Christ, compared with your BC life?

MODERN-DAY TESTIMONIES

The BC-Cross-AD formula worked well for Paul and continues to serve the same purpose today. Let's look at two modern-day testimonies as proof.

Dennis Tells His Story

In the previous two chapters of this book, I mentioned my friend Dennis, who leads a small group of third-grade boys every Sunday. When he tells his story, he combines the three-part outline with the four communication dynamics covered in chapter 2 to deliver a testimony kids love.

BC

"Hey guys, I'd love to tell you a story about a young guy who was about eight years old. He loved to play baseball, soccer, and especially basketball. Now he wasn't the best kid on the team all the time and he didn't always get picked first, but when he played, he played really hard. He also went to church almost every week and learned lots of stories in the Bible.

"One day there was a story about how Jesus had to die on the cross and he didn't even deserve to. So after church this young guy told his mom about the story. She asked if he would like to talk to the pastor to hear more about the story. The little guy said okay.

"He was kind of nervous, but he still went and sat down to talk with the pastor. He found out the pastor was really a pretty good guy, and that it was pretty comfortable to talk with him. The pastor asked if he had ever done anything that his mom and dad had not wanted him to do. Well, he couldn't really lie to the pastor, so he said yes. The pastor said that those are what God calls sins. And that's why Jesus had to do what he did—it was to get rid of all our sins. The pastor asked him if he would like to pray about his sin now. And the boy said okay, but he was really nervous. The pastor started praying, but noticed that this little boy wasn't praying with him. So the pastor asked God to help the boy come to know him more."

The Cross

"Well, that guy continued going to church for a long time, and he continued to play basketball and did stuff like the rest of the guys. As a matter of fact, one day he ended up being the captain of his basketball team. His small group leader was there for one game, and after it was over, he explained to a group of boys that in the Bible it says we need to go and talk to Jesus and ask him to be our friend. And nobody can do that for us. Immediately, the boy thought back to the time when he was sitting with the pastor, and how the pastor prayed he would become a good friend of God. He realized he had never really told Jesus himself that he needed to be forgiven for all he had done wrong. So right then, he prayed with his small group leader for Jesus to be his friend, for Jesus to forgive him, and for Jesus to make sure he could go to heaven one day."

AD

"From that point on, this guy knew that Jesus would always be with him, and that he was going to spend forever in heaven.

"The reason I tell you guys this story is that I know it's true. I know it's true because this is my story. You see, after talking with my small group leader I understood that all I had to do was pray to start a real friendship with Jesus. And that's what I did. If you are ready to pray to Jesus, I'd love to do that with you just like my small group leader did with me. But if you're not ready yet, that's okay too. We can spend as much time as you want talking about this to help you really figure it out for yourself."

My Testimony

I've had several opportunities to relate my own story during Promiseland salvation weekends, while talking with my own children, and in conversations with other adults. The three paragraphs that follow contain the words I'm likely to say after "Here's what happened to me."

BC

"I grew up going to church every weekend where I heard a lot about the Bible. Have you ever had to learn a lot about something, but you really didn't understand what it meant? I admit that I really didn't see the need to care about what happened to people so long ago. And because of that attitude, God seemed to be a long way from my world. That belief, unfortunately, allowed me to do a lot of stuff that I knew wasn't right. Who cared about a God who was way, way out there when I wasn't getting caught doing wrong stuff right here? For many years—until I was twenty-nine—my life was a lot of fun high points followed by difficult low times."

The Cross

"Then a couple that my wife and I hung out with invited us to a church. At first we went so that we'd have a place to go at Christmas and Easter because we didn't have a church of our own to attend. But we liked that church, and decided to keep going each week. Then one Sunday, I heard a message about God wanting to have a personal relationship with individual people—even people like me. For the first time in my life, I understood what a relationship with God meant, and it sounded good to me. I heard that I could start this friendship by just praying to Jesus, so I did."

AD

"And now, guess what? I still have good times and not so good times, but that's okay because Jesus is with me no matter what, just like a best friend. I love living every day amazed and grateful that he is close to someone like me—guiding me, helping me, and loving me."

TELLING YOUR OWN STORY

We should highlight two key points about testimonies. First, both stories you just read definitely qualify as child-appropriate, but would likely change if used with grown-ups. When I share my testimony with other adults, I typically add details in the BC and AD eras that bring clarity to my highs and lows. But because I filter my comments through the four communication dynamics, especially regarding details that might distract, I employ a different approach with kids. The essence of my story, though, remains unchanged.

> People who experience salvation at a
> very young age might wonder if the
> BC-Cross-AD approach will work for them.

Second, people who experience salvation at a very young age might wonder if the BC-Cross-AD approach will work for them. If you fall into this category, then I believe you have an advantage over those of us saved later in life. The fact that at a young age you made the decision to become a Christian establishes strong common ground with your listeners. So unapologetically include statements that begin with "When I was about your age ...," "Something cool happened to me when I was six ...," or other words that allow you to go back and be a kid again.

The Short Story

Whether your story is from your childhood or a more recent period, the length will pose a challenge. If you were to write your testimony this moment, there's a strong likelihood that you would join Dennis and me with a version as long as Acts 26. Chances are also good that you'd never remember it. So don't start writing yet. We're going to simplify.

Fortunately, the apostle Paul helps us once again. In Galatians 1:13–17, he shares a much shorter conversion story:

For you have heard of my previous way of life in Judaism, how intensely I persecuted the church of God and tried to destroy it. I was advancing in Judaism beyond many Jews of my own age and was extremely zealous for the traditions of my fathers. But when God, who set me apart from birth and called me by his grace, was pleased to reveal his Son in me so that I might preach him among the Gentiles, I did not consult any man, nor did I go up to Jerusalem to see those who were apostles before I was, but I went immediately into Arabia and later returned to Damascus.

Paul's narrative in Galatians 1 tells the same story as Acts 26, yet in a condensed version. To prove the transferability of such a condensation to modern-day stories, we'll look at

Dennis's and my testimonies in a four-sentence format. If a child (or adult!) has a short attention span or if a brief moment is all that's available, then the compact version might be all you have time to say.

Dennis's Story Shortened

1. When I was a kid, I went to church every Sunday and learned all about Jesus and the Bible.
2. I even had the pastor of our church pray with me that I would follow Jesus.
3. But when I was older, someone helped me understand that I needed to pray for myself to follow Jesus and ask him to forgive my sins, which is what I did.
4. And now I know Jesus is my friend and that someday I will be with him in heaven.

My Story Shortened

1. Growing up, I went to church for many years and heard a lot about the Bible, but it didn't seem important and God seemed far away from me.
2. When I was twenty-nine, though, I learned that God wants to have a personal relationship with everyone, including me.
3. All I had to do was pray to start this friendship with Jesus, so I did.
4. And today I'm just amazed I get to live life knowing that he is close by—guiding me, helping me, and loving me.

You Can Do It Too

While training a large room of children's ministry workers I asked Megan, a student helper in our ministry, to share her story just like she does with younger kids. The enthusiastic response to her words galvanized the audience's belief that brevity can have impact. I suspect hearing a young person comfortably articulate her story convinced everyone that they too could develop their own four sentences.

1. I started going to Promiseland when I was in second grade.
2. I had a really nice leader who answered a lot of my questions.
3. Finally, in fourth grade, I admitted that I sin and believed that Jesus died for my sins.
4. Then I asked Jesus to be my forever friend—and he still is.

Megan shows us that describing a journey to finding faith can be a simple story. Angie Walker from First Reformed Church in Grandville, Michigan, agrees:

> This training made me realize the importance of sharing my testimony with everyone—young and old. It also made me realize that my testimony doesn't need to—and shouldn't—be complicated. Keeping it simple is the key.

Most people can remember four sentences, especially when the topic is themselves. The first step is to put pencil to paper. So after you finish reading this chapter, write four sentences that capture your story of becoming a Christian.

Start with each era's key words that you jotted down earlier. Then add details as needed. For now, though, focus on fashioning four sentences that will easily come to mind when needed. Once done, you can share your testimony any time. And with the reality of attention spans, four sentences might be all you get. So give it all you've got while you write. Additional four-sentence examples appear at the end of this chapter.

Filter

Don't forget to apply the four communication dynamics from the previous chapter to keep the language of your story kid-friendly. To filter your story with the dynamics, refer to these questions while you write:

BC

1. Is this a condition or lifestyle to which a child can relate? If no, then simplify.
2. Will a child be distracted by my sinful past or lifestyle details? If yes, then reword or delete.

The Cross

1. Is it clear that I took some action when I accepted Christ? If no, think more specifically.

2. Is what I did understandable and applicable to a child? If no, then reword.

AD

1. Is the change Christ made in my life easy to understand? If no, then describe the change differently, or focus on a different type of change.
2. Do I make description of my life as a Christian clear to a child? If no, then simplify by using words kids might say when they describe aspects of life.

Refine

To strengthen your story further, consider Paul's shortest testimony in Galatians 1:23. Using limited words, he acknowledges that he used to persecute the church and now proclaims their faith. Or look in John 9 at the man who says that he was once blind and now he sees. Both of these one-sentence descriptions show the marked difference between BC life and AD life. "Persecute" becomes "proclaim." "Blind" becomes "I see." Why? Jesus made the difference. Structure your story so that it too shows identifiable life change.

> Structure your story so that it shows identifiable life change.

Organizing your story and refining it into four easy-to-remember sentences requires effort, so expect the process to take time. Clarity will emerge from a crisp account of your faith journey; overexplaining and rambling will cloud over it. As Philippe de Commynes, a late fifteenth-century writer, said, "One never repents of having spoken too little, but often of having spoken too much."[4]

The Payoff

The first time your four sentences come to mind at an opportune moment, the effort you invest now will pay off—for you and for whoever listens to you. Peggy Rice, a former student of training on this topic who now teaches others in Wisconsin to do the same, sees this exercise as a confidence builder:

> By putting my story in four sentences, it has helped me "demystify" the whole "testimony" thing. It's so cool to be able to tell women at my table that they don't need to be intimidated by "writing their testimony"—all they need to do is put their story of their relationship with Jesus on paper. And then I encourage them to do it in four sentences so that a child can understand. The word "testimony" can seem so scary, but when we talk about it as really just the story about what God is doing or has done in your life, it makes it easier.

Since our family returned from Disney World, many friends have asked about our trip—what we liked, what we would do differently, and whether Space Mountain is really a thrill. All these inquisitive people seem to take the stories we share about our visit to heart. A few go so far as to tell us they plan to duplicate the activities and follow the strategies that we recommend. We didn't need to write a book about our experiences, all we needed to do was say, "Here's what happened to us...." There's just no substitute for a personal testimony.

And the first step toward yours is just four sentences away.

Personal Exercises

1. Write your story:

My Story

    1. _____

    _____

    2. _____

    _____

    3. _____

    _____

    4. _____

    _____

2. Read your four sentences aloud and time yourself. If it's longer than one minute, cut down your sentence length.

3. Share your four sentences with at least two other adults. Ask for feedback on clarity. Make changes as needed.

Additional Examples of Four-Sentence Testimonies

Peggy
Madison, WI

1. Before I became a Christian, I went to Sunday school and played nicely with my sister and my friends and I was a good girl.

2. But I learned from the Bible that I couldn't go to heaven just because I was a good kid!

3. So I asked Jesus to forgive the wrong things that I had done and to be my friend forever.

4. And now I know that one day, I will be in heaven with Jesus forever, that Jesus will always be with me and help me every day, and I can learn more about him by reading the Bible and praying to him.

Angie
Grandville, MI

1. I grew up going to church and Sunday school but I didn't live the way Jesus wanted me to live.

2. When I was in fifth grade something scary and lonely happened to me.

3. I then realized that the only way I could make it through this scary and lonely time would be to accept Jesus.

4. Since then I don't feel lonely or scared because I know Jesus is my friend.

Gary
Peoria, IL

1. My parents loved me so much that they took me to church every week.

2. For many years I heard that Jesus wanted to be my friend.

3. One night, I realized that I needed to invite Jesus into my life to be my friend. My mom prayed with me after church.

4. Now, I live each day knowing that Jesus is my friend, and I will live with him forever.

Alistair
Cape Town, South Africa

1. I used to swear too much, didn't show respect toward other people, and didn't go to church.

2. One day last year I was invited by friends to church and really enjoyed it.

3. I realized that I needed to change, and I gave my life to Jesus.

4. Since doing this, my life has become better, I've made more friends, I treat others with more respect, and I control what I say.

CHAPTER 4

Share God's Story

S ome plans seem too good to be true. My son Scott likely felt that way when he heard the plan for our day together each time we walked into a popular amusement park north of Chicago. The concept was easy to understand: "Today we'll do anything you want to do—everything is your choice."

Scott loved hearing those words every year. Kids live a life filled with limited choices—ride a swing or go down a slide, bologna or peanut butter and jelly, homework before dinner or right after. Imagine the thrill of walking toward a giant playground full of the coolest stuff you've ever seen, with a parent who's all yours for a whole day, and hearing you're in charge. Of course I knew that one admission price paid for all the rides, so I wasn't at significant financial risk. Or was I?

One year we arrived at 9:45 a.m. and rushed through the gates when they opened at 10:00. Once inside, a newly empowered Scott announced our first activity and off we went. Ten minutes later we sat down. At a table. To eat an ice cream cone. But not just any cone—this was a seven-dollar dairy masterpiece nearly as large as my head! I frantically scanned the price of other foods I knew he loved, and calculated that financial ruin was very possible by noon. I had to think fast because the risk was real that my wallet would melt as quickly as the ice cream. Then the idea came to me: battle his appetite.

"This must be the world's largest ice cream cone," I said. "Do you think we can eat it all?" Filled with a purpose, we ate for the next thirty minutes. Actually, I made sure Scott did most of the eating. And after a heroic effort that required more than twenty napkins, we declared the cone as winner because it still held about two dollars' worth of vanilla-chocolate swirl. Maybe co-winner is a better word—I shared the victory because Scott couldn't eat another thing for more than two hours.

The reason for this story is not to illustrate the potential dangers posed by adults who allow kids to make nutritional decisions. Nor is it a lesson on cash management. The point is this—Scott heard a great plan and opted to take advantage of it. To do so, he had to understand the plan I explained to him, and he had to see how it personally applied to him.

In a similar fashion, kids need to hear about the greatest plan—the gospel plan of salvation through Jesus Christ. And although the plan makes perfect sense to Christian adults, explaining it in ways that kids will personally understand can present a big challenge. Without forethought and preparation, a salvation explanation could easily sound like it's delivered in a foreign tongue.

A few years ago my wife and I served on a mission trip to an orphanage in Baja California, Mexico. Each day we joined child evangelism teams that visited camps filled with kids left to fend for themselves as adults and older siblings worked in area tomato fields. These beautiful kids loved seeing the orphanage vans filled with adults; they knew that the sole reason for our trip was to visit with them.

Regrettably, my Spanish fluency consisted of questions about age and the location of the nearest bathroom. Because of this language deficiency, my task list included the following:

> Although the plan of salvation makes perfect sense to Christian adults, explaining it in ways that kids will personally understand can present a big challenge.

(1) drive the van, (2) carry supplies, (3) set up a small area for the Bible study, and (4) let kids climb on me. Oh yes, and smile. After just a few short minutes, I knew everyone's age and the locations of several bathrooms. Then the real teachers took over.

"Jesus is willing to always be with you" is a comforting message to kids left alone each day until they're old enough for field work. But considering the audience, I would never have dreamed of trying to convey Jesus' message in English. These bright-eyed kids needed to hear it in words they could personally understand. In similar fashion, children's ministry workers and parents face a challenge to explain the greatest message in the world using terms that make sense to kids.

KID-TALK BASICS

Fortunately, sharing the salvation plan with children does not require you to learn a second language. In fact, just as you worked with your testimony in the previous chapter, we'll work on developing basic kid-talk that involves simple and familiar terms. To do this requires two considerations: First, know the story to tell. Second, use the right words.

Know the Story to Tell

Don serves as a small group leader in our third-grade room. During large group time, our ministry periodically presents the gospel plan of salvation. The week after one such presentation, Don noticed that three boys who missed the previous week were back in his group. He asked his co-leader to take the rest of the group into the worship time while he stayed back with just those three. Over the next few minutes, he explained the message they had missed. After his explanation, all three prayed to start a relationship with Jesus.

Kudos for Don! But if you were in his shoes, do you have confidence that you would know what to say and how to say it?

Check your local bookstore or search the Internet and you'll find entire books, videos, and websites that communicate what it means to be a Christian. But while you can share a book or other materials with an adult, interacting with a child requires different preparation—because the window of opportunity to address a kid's interest opens and shuts quickly. To that end, your challenge is to know the basic tenets of faith so you can clearly share them in a minute or two. Sometimes you'll have more time. Sometimes you'll have less. But regardless of the time available, knowing the basics is the place to start.

The *Becoming a Contagious Christian* evangelism training course suggests remembering the gospel using a four-part outline:

1. God
2. Us
3. Christ
4. You and me

Armed with the four components of God's story, you can share them whenever and however the need arises. Popular gospel illustrations such as the Bridge, the Wordless Book, and other tools are—at their core—clever deliveries of this same message. Craig Jutila, children's pastor at Saddleback Church in Lake Forest, California, provides wise coaching to children's ministries when he says, "The message doesn't change; just the method."[1]

Before we examine method, though, let's fully understand the message—segmented into the *Becoming a Contagious Christian* four-part format.

1. God

- He is a holy God, perfect in every way. Nothing else in this world fits the description of being perfect, so everything will fall short in a comparison to God. Yet, he created people to be like himself, along with an expectation of holiness or perfection.

  Be holy because I, the Lord your God, am holy.
  Leviticus 19:2

- He is a loving God, who loves each of us more than we can imagine. In fact, God created love.

  We love because he first loved us.
  1 John 4:19

- He is a just God, so he doesn't turn the other way and ignore sin.

  For I the Lord love justice; I hate robbery and wrongdoing.
  Isaiah 61:8 (NRSV)

2. Us

- All people commit sin. And when compared to God's beautiful standard of perfection, sin paints an ugly picture of a person.

  For all have sinned and fall short of the glory of God.
  Romans 3:23

- The debt each person accumulates from sin results in only one suitable payment, which is death—both physical and spiritual. This spiritual death is complete separation from God for eternity.

  The wages of sin is death.

  Romans 6:23

- No matter how hard we try, we could never offer enough of a sacrifice to clear away all our sins. But someone has to.

  "The multitude of your sacrifices — what are they to me?" says the Lord.

  Isaiah 1:11

3. *Christ*

- Jesus Christ is God who became man and lived on earth.

  In the beginning was the Word, and the Word was with God, and the Word was God. . . . The Word became flesh and made his dwelling among us.

  John 1:1, 14

- Even though he never committed any sins, Christ died as our substitute—willfully punished for sins we commit. Following his sacrificial crucifixion came Christ's resurrection, which shows he has power over death. Christianity is faith in someone who still lives.

  But God demonstrates his own love for us in this: While we were still sinners, Christ died for us.

  Romans 5:8

  I am the Living One; I was dead, and behold I am alive for ever and ever! And I hold the keys of death and Hades.

  Revelation 1:18

- And Christ as our Savior offers us complete forgiveness for all our sins as a free gift.

  For all have sinned and fall short of the glory of God, and are justified freely by his grace through the redemption that came by Christ Jesus.

  Romans 3:23–24

  For it is by grace you have been saved, through faith — and this not from yourselves, it is the gift of God.

  Ephesians 2:8

4. You and Me

- The free gift of salvation must be accepted through a personal response to the gospel. We must ask Jesus into our heart as Lord and Savior, and the Leader of our lives.

  That if you confess with your mouth, "Jesus is Lord," and believe in your heart that God raised him from the dead, you will be saved.

  Romans 10:9

  Be very careful, then, how you live — not as unwise but as wise. . . . Therefore do not be foolish, but understand what the Lord's will is.

  Ephesians 5:15, 17

- At that moment, we become adopted into God's family.

  Yet to all who received him, to those who believed in his name, he gave the right to become children of God.

  John 1:12

- Because of Christ's presence in us, spiritual transformation takes place.

  Therefore, if anyone is in Christ, he is a new creation; the old has gone, the new has come!

  2 Corinthians 5:17

Use the Right Words

The explanation for the gospel that we just went through, while perfectly understandable to an adult, would earn a very low kid-friendly rating based on my word choices. Abstract phrases abound, as does language that will fly past kids at the speed of sound.

Rewording the gospel—is that legal? Yes. Our language provides us with word options that do an excellent job of preserving its meaning. The entire reason to explain the gospel is in hopes that a child will make a life-changing decision based on personally understanding and believing God's plan. For that to happen, complex vocabulary comprehension should not exist as a prerequisite to the free gift of grace. Without kid-friendly words, any salvation explanation collapses—even the time-honored Bridge will seem to be an odd stick-figure drawing and the Wordless Book will fall on innocently deaf ears.

> Rewording the gospel—is that legal? Yes. Our language provides us with word options that do an excellent job of preserving its meaning.

Acts 14:1 states the need for—and benefit of—sharing the salvation plan in listener-focused language: "At Iconium Paul and Barnabas went as usual into the Jewish synagogue. There they spoke so effectively that a great number of Jews and Gentiles believed." The original Greek words translate into "spoke in a manner." Paul didn't alter the meaning or message of the gospel; he simply modified his verbal delivery to accommodate his listeners. The words "great number of Jews and Gentiles" indicate that this approach yielded significant success.

In 1 Corinthians, Paul reveals that this manner-modifying approach became a deliberate strategy that stretched past Iconium:

To the Jews I became like a Jew, to win the Jews. To those under the law I became like one under the law (though I myself am not under the law), so as to win those under the law. To those not having the law I became like one not having the law (though I am not free from God's law but am under Christ's law), so as to win those not having the law. To the weak I became weak, to win the weak. I have become all things to all men so that by all possible means I might save some. I do all this for the sake of the gospel, that I may share in its blessings.

(1 Corinthians 9:20–23)

The gospel Paul shared in the first century with residents of what is now Konya, Turkey, and beyond is the same gospel message that we share with children in the twenty-first century. And just as they did in Paul's day, the words we use deserve attention.

KID-TALK FLUENCY

To start, we'll pull out key words from the four-part gospel description above. Then we'll find child-appropriate words that preserve the biblical message. To make this easy, the chart that follows provides kid-friendly terms that bring strong, yet simple meaning to a handful of common terms used frequently by adults. However, the right-hand column is not in the same order as the left, so take a moment and draw lines between the synonymous phrases. An answer key follows.

Common terms	**Kid-friendly terms**
1. Sin	A. Someone who agrees to be in trouble for us
2. Punishment	B. Killed on a cross because we're in so much trouble
3. Crucified	C. Follow what Jesus says, ask him for help to do the right thing
4. Savior	D. Ask Jesus to forgive you and always be your friend
5. Resurrected	E. Not nice, wrong things we do
6. Ask Jesus into your heart	F. Get in trouble, time-out, spanking
7. Let Jesus be Lord	G. Didn't stay dead

(1-E, 2-F, 3-B, 4-A, 5-G, 6-D, 7-C)

Notice that the kid-friendly phrases share the same meaning as the common terms; they just use commonsense word choices that focus on young listeners. You have to admit, if you tell a kid that the blood of the lamb will wash away sins, she will think you are pretty gross. But if you say that Jesus offers to be in trouble for all the wrong stuff we do, you stand a good chance at capturing some attention. While the manner can be modified, the meaning stays the same. And maybe a life changes as a result.

Common sense dictates that different ages will require different words. The key to success is the willingness to throw religious-sounding words out the window and to modify your terminology. So brainstorm a little. Pray and ask God to help you bring new words to mind. You need only a few to make the story, his story, clear to a kid. What age children are you around most? What cultural considerations will influence your word choice? Create a list of terms and phrases likely to resonate well with your kids.

A team of communicators from our children's ministry developed the following list to prompt your thinking:

Sin	things we do wrong, bad things we do, no-no's, mistakes, naughty stuff, when we disobey, make bad choices, things we do that make God sad
Punishment	get grounded/time-out/spanking/have to stay in room, consequences, penalty, get in trouble, be disciplined
Crucified	died on a cross because that person was in so much trouble, killed, hurt bad and then died
Savior	forever friend, rescuer, helper, took bad stuff for us, agrees to be in trouble instead of you, took our place, was hurt and killed even though he did nothing wrong
Resurrection	alive again, came back from being dead, didn't stay dead, came back to life
Ask Jesus into your heart	follow Jesus, become a Christian, become best friends with Jesus, start a relationship with Jesus, tell Jesus you're sorry and ask him to always be your friend
Lord or Leader of my life	let Jesus show me the right/best way to live, let Jesus help you make right choices, Jesus helps me do the right things, a guide, have Jesus as the one I follow and obey, someone who will always listen/care/help
Ask for forgiveness	say you're sorry, apologize
Forgiveness	not in trouble anymore
Confess	admit you did wrong, tell what you did
Eternal life	live forever in heaven with Jesus

Now imagine what the gospel message might sound like when using child-centered terms. The following explanation (originally used by an adult in our church as a response to a girl's question "How do you get to heaven?") will stimulate your imagination:

Do you remember how God can do everything and see everything? Well, that means he can see all the things we do, even the things that aren't nice. He also knows when we are saying stuff that isn't nice, and even when we're not thinking nice things. All of that really disappoints God because he doesn't think it's okay for us to do anything wrong. Can you imagine all the wrong stuff you or I do? No matter if we get caught or not, it means we should be in a lot of trouble.

So much trouble that one day when we die, we wouldn't be allowed in heaven. That would be sad, wouldn't it?

But that's where Jesus helps us out. He never did anything wrong, but he still agreed to be in trouble with God for all the things that we did wrong. It's like he agreed to take all the spankings and time-outs for what other people have done. Can you imagine how many that would be? Do you know how he had to do it? He had to actually die hanging on a cross. But he didn't stay dead, which is how he can be with us today. And the real good news is that what he did will count for all the bad things you and I do. All we have to do is ask him to forgive us and to always be our friend, and to help us figure out how to do good stuff. Want to know how to do that?

Susan Shadid, who oversees Promiseland's training program and contributes valuable expertise to curriculum content, suggests adding a reference to joining God's family when explaining the salvation plan. "Children possess a universal longing to belong, so the very real opportunity to be part of a family appeals to many kids," she explains.

> Consider specific word changes in the language you naturally use to explain prayer, baptism, communion, church attendance, volunteerism, and other common aspects of church life.

After you consider new words that will increase kids' comprehension of the gospel message, then turn your attention to other aspects of Christianity and Bible stories that might confuse children. That list may well be fairly long. To put this idea in practice, consider specific word changes in the language you naturally use to explain prayer, baptism, communion, church attendance, volunteerism, and other common aspects of church life. This isn't an exercise in rewording established doctrine—it's to achieve a kid-friendly explanation. Then do the same for a Bible story or two.

It's Still His Story and His Timing

Our family spends a few morning moments together reading the Bible. As I was writing this chapter, we were partway through Matthew when my daughter asked me about the Roman commander in Matthew 8 whose servant receives long-distance healing from Jesus. "I don't get that story," said seven-year-old Erin. So I offered this explanation:

"The Roman soldier believes that Jesus has the power to heal, which means to make sick people feel better. He even believes that Jesus is so powerful that he can heal anyone just by saying 'Be healed.' The Roman soldier is an important guy, who gives other people orders they have to follow. So he tells Jesus that he believes Jesus has the same ability to give an order—no matter what it is—and it will be done. Even something like healing a sick person. Jesus was pretty impressed that this real important Roman guy believed in Jesus' power to do stuff—which meant the Roman had faith in Jesus. So when we talk about having faith in Jesus, we really mean that we believe in Jesus' power and that he can do anything. Jesus said that because the Roman had lots of faith, he would heal the Roman's servant. And you know what? Later on in the Bible, Jesus says if we have that same kind of faith in him, then he'll answer *our* prayers."

And the story gets even better. Erin seemed to understand the concept of faith fairly well, thanks to that story in Matthew 8:5–13. I drew that conclusion because of her summary. She said, "So if faith is believing in Jesus' power, then maybe I should say more prayers to him when I get scared of storms." Imagine how huge her eyes became, and how hard my heart pounded, when the very next day we started reading at verse 23—the story of Jesus calming the storm!

I could not have planned that sequence of stories any better, nor am I foolish enough to think I should try. The same truth applies to modifying our manner of language to share the gospel with kids. We will not consider changing words to fit our expectations of what the gospel should be or what the Bible "ought to" say. We will, though, change the words we use to make God's story, his plan, more accessible to kids. Because the only way a plan has strong appeal is when it's understood.

The plan, of course, is God's rather than ours. Even though we deliver the message, true comprehension and conviction comes solely as a result of the Holy Spirit. To that end, no matter how well we word the gospel, different kids will require different quantities of time to fully understand. Give them as much as they need.

> Even though we deliver the message, true comprehension and conviction comes solely as a result of the Holy Spirit.

At the start of this chapter, I shared my son Scott's delight when he heard about an incredible, we'll-do-anything-you-want plan in place during amusement park visits every summer. A piece of the story I didn't share earlier is that he waited until the second year to fully take advantage of the plan and order the mountain of ice cream. Similarly, it may take awhile before a child decides he is ready to do something about the world's *greatest* plan. And you will want to be ready. Because when that day comes, you don't want to let the opportunity melt away.

Personal Exercises

1. On the chart below, fill in kid-friendly and age-appropriate terms that will connect best with the children in your ministry setting:

Sin	
Punishment	
Crucified	
Savior	
Resurrection	
Ask Jesus into your heart	
Lord or Leader of my life	
Ask for forgiveness	
Forgiveness	
Confess	
Eternal life	

2. On one side of a small note card list the four parts of the salvation plan. (You'll need the other side of the note card in chapter 5. For some people, adding this as a memo to your PDA might work better than a physical card.) Next to each point, write a short sentence of explanation. Always carry this reminder so you can refresh your memory prior to any situation in which you might need to share God's story (with kids or adults).

3. Practice explaining the salvation plan with at least two other adults. Ask for feedback on clarity and kid-friendliness.

CHAPTER 5

The Prayer and Beyond

Anticipation built like water collecting behind a dam. Our family had wanted to ride the bumper cars at a local amusement park, but the line stretched so long we decided to keep walking. "We'll come back a little later so we don't waste time waiting," I assured my son. We passed the hours engaged in activities that delivered less fun, knowing that eventually the line would shorten and our decision to delay satisfaction would pay off. To our pleasant surprise, we discovered a unique advantage to small amusement parks—all attractions are scaled down in size, meaning the fear factor is low and so is the minimum height requirement to ride. All, that is, except for one.

Bumper cars deliver a unique flavor of fun. What starts as a group of people stepping into cute little cars painted in bright primary colors quickly changes into twenty-four heavy projectiles intentionally crashing into each other. It's a bump-or-be-bumped experience, and the objective is the harder the better. The world is a different place on the bumper car ride for several reasons.

THE SEVEN WONDERS OF BUMPER CARS

1. For unknown reasons, dads change when they sit in bumper cars and become the roughhousing, out-to-hurt-someone person they don't tolerate back home.

2. Unbelievably, a wad of bubble gum will not short out the electrical grate above the cars—the power source that supplies the current to make everything run.

3. For three minutes, just for fun, mature adults deliberately build up speed for twenty feet and slam cars that carry their entire body weight into cars driven by ten-year-old children.

4. An interesting ride feature is that if the steering wheel is turned far enough the car will move in reverse. This does not work in real automobiles and takes more than three minutes for some people to learn.

5. There's always one passive person who naively tries to avoid contact with other cars, thus becoming a high-priority target for the dads.

6. Total strangers will form unspoken, sinister alliances in less than ten seconds to terrorize that passive person until the ride ends—and it never ends quickly.

7. The ride will be shut down immediately when one is escorted from a bumper car for throwing bubble gum at the electrical grate.

After the crowd thinned, our family arrived at the bumper car line. Common sense told us that our three-year-old daughter was much too young, so she and my wife sat down nearby. That left Scott and me, the boys, to defend the family name on the bumper car battlefield. Our spirits soared as we approached the turnstile.

Although I felt prepared to encounter and overcome the wonder-filled world we were set to enter, unfortunately we encountered an unexpected problem. The top of Scott's head measured less than an inch short of the minimum height to ride.

We experienced shock and awe. Shock at the fact that only one measuring stick in this entire park eliminated Scott—from the ride we most wanted to go on, no less. The awe came when I said, "Awe, c'mon. He's so close!" The high school–aged attendant just shook his head. Mine lowered.

Then Scott spoke up. "What about you, Dad?" he said. "Aren't you big enough?"

"Of course I am, buddy," I said, "but I'm not going to just leave you out." (I admit that option did momentarily flash through my mind.)

"No, Dad," he said. "I mean you're big enough to make that guy let me on!"

Don't worry—I didn't try to overpower the hired hand. He was just doing his job. But that experience did help me realize once again that there are some things an adult simply can't do for a child. Obviously, I had no power to make my son tall enough for that ride. He had to do that for himself.

In similar fashion, adults can't start a child's personal relationship with Jesus. Oh, we might want to—all parents want the best for their kids, and Sunday school teachers and small group leaders spend hours praying for children. But despite the presence and influence of adults with God-honoring intentions, every child must decide on his or her own to cross the line of faith. And that's the focus of this chapter—helping kids take the crucial step to accept Christ as Lord and Savior. With simple preparation on our parts, we can ensure that the last step doesn't include any major bumps.

> But despite the presence and influence of adults with God-honoring intentions, every child must decide on his or her own to cross the line of faith.

HELPING KIDS TAKE THE FINAL STEP

What moment are we preparing for? The one in which a kid asks about what he needs to do to become a Christian. Of course the question doesn't always sound the same, and the circumstances surrounding it promise to be unpredictable. But the outcome can be incredible, as my friend Carla affirms in a story involving her five-year-old daughter.

> Alyssandra and I had been watching videos about the book of Matthew, and as a result, she had a lot of questions. She wanted to know why people didn't like Jesus. When I explained why and what he stood for, she asked if I believed in Jesus. I told her yes. Then she asked me if I was going to heaven. I told her yes, that I had prayed to accept Christ. I then explained the steps of the prayer.
>
> She said to me, "I love Jesus; I want Jesus to live in my heart. Will you help me pray that prayer?" I was so excited—I had tears in my eyes!
>
> So we prayed together, about eight o'clock at night, driving on a highway on December 14. I still remember the light of the moon shining on her little face as she sat in the backseat.

Carla feels fortunate that she knew how to explain the prayer of salvation. And in time, I imagine Alyssandra will feel grateful too. To make the most of any opportunity that might come our way, whether on a highway lit by the moon or in a hallway on Sunday morning, let's get to work at understanding the prayer. We'll start by looking in the Bible.

Scripture to Guide Our Journey

In Acts 2:37, a large group of people heard the story of Jesus and someone asked the disciples, "Brothers, what shall we do?" Fourteen chapters later, in Acts 16:30, the Roman jailer asked Paul and Silas nearly the same question: "Sirs, what must I do to be saved?" The responses in both situations lay the foundation for how we should help children who ask similar questions.

Acts 2:38 records Peter telling the group to repent. Acts 16:31 shows Paul and Silas responding to the jailer with "Believe in the Lord Jesus." Both examples give clear direction that an internalization of the salvation message needs to take place. To *repent* requires me to personally acknowledge that I've done wrong, while to *believe* starts with a personal conviction that something is true or reliable. And the Bible has more to say about being saved.

Romans 10:9 provides excellent coaching for what a person must do for salvation, "If you confess with your mouth, 'Jesus is Lord,' and believe in your heart that God raised him from the dead, you will be saved." As does Matthew 10:32 (NRSV), "Everyone therefore who acknowledges me before others, I also will acknowledge before my Father in heaven." The same Greek word appears for "confess" and "acknowledge"—with the root word meaning that something is stated. Both these verses point us to the role words play in turning one's life over to Christ.

Combine these four passages (Acts 2:37–38; 16:30–31; Romans 10:9; Matthew 10:32), and the need for a prayer—something stated—becomes apparent. Some Christ-followers may debate whether or not the prayer must be said aloud for others to hear, but that's not the point. What's truly important for our discussion is that we have the opportunity to help a child cross the line of faith if we can assist them in saying a prayer. For simplicity's sake, we'll assume the child speaks the words.

Words for an A-B-C Salvation Prayer

But what words? Let's go back to Acts to find out. *Repenting of sins* emerges as important, which involves admitting my sins and asking for forgiveness. *Believing on the Lord Jesus* means to understand that he died for my sins and rose again, and that he must become the Lord—or leader—of my life. Not exactly kid-friendly words yet, so let's continue to work on them. If the salvation prayer is to serve as a basic tool that anyone involved with children can use, then it should be as easy to remember as A-B-C.

The origin of using A-B-C for the salvation prayer in children's ministry is obscure, but its simplicity is quite evident. Remember those three letters and you can help anyone—young or old—pray to become a Christian.

A—Admit your sins and ask for forgiveness.
B—Believe in Jesus and that he died for your sins.
C—Choose to follow Jesus the rest of your life.

In second grade, Sarah decided she had heard enough about God to make a decision. She vividly remembers the morning in her children's ministry when she became a Christian:

> I already knew some stuff about God, and I knew it [following Christ] was an important decision. So I decided to wait until I was older to take that step.

Finally in second grade, I felt like I really understood and wanted to have a relationship with Jesus. The A-B-C prayer just made so much sense to me. I prayed it after hearing an adult describe how she became a Christian; her story was a big deal to me.

It's important for kids to see a special look in their leader's eyes when he or she [the leader] talks about Jesus. And after the prayer, I felt like I had that look, too. The whole day felt like something big just happened.

Something big did happen for Sarah that day, catalyzed by something as simple as A-B-C. Sarah was clearly ready to take the step of praying for salvation, but such clarity isn't always the case. Due to the eternal stakes involved with this prayer, it is important to follow three simple guidelines that address common questions about whether or not a child is ready to enter a relationship with Christ.

Simple Guidelines on Readiness

First, make sure the child possesses a genuine, personal desire to pray. If a group setting exists, peer pressure can, unfortunately, result in misguided motivation. An adult (you) can also unduly influence a child to pray as a means of pleasing a parent or small group leader. Sensitivity to both situations will enable your discernment as to whether or not the Holy Spirit is at work—in a child-sized way, of course. Simply saying a prayer is not what we're after; it must be sincere. And in most cases, one easy question delivered in a gentle tone will reveal the motivation behind why a kid wants to ask Jesus into her life: "Can you tell me why you want to do this?"

After posing the question, remain quiet until the child offers a response. If it's no, then review the salvation plan (see chapter 4) and ask questions along the way to create an open dialogue in which the child feels safe to admit any confusion. For example, "Over the last week, have you done anything that you knew was wrong to do, even if you weren't caught?"

If she has a reason for asking Jesus into her life that makes age-appropriate sense, then prompt the child through the A-B-C prayer.

Second, don't discount a child's desire to pray for salvation on more than one occasion. Chris, now a teenager, looks back at his faith journey and appreciates the flexibility and understanding shown by his small group leaders:

> I prayed the A-B-C prayer for the first time in third grade. But the next year, my small group leader explained more concepts about being a Christian, so I decided to pray again. Then my next small group leader showed our group how to put even more parts of following Jesus into motion. He made everything so easy to understand with how he described stuff, so I said the A-B-C prayer again.
>
> My understanding of this commitment grew each year, which is why I kept praying. Life gets more intense each year—especially in sixth grade, so I just wanted to be sure.

Fortunately, no one ever gave Chris the sense that what he was doing was wrong or unnecessary. If a kid more fully understands salvation this month or this year and wants to pray again, or possibly just wants to be sure about the issue, your guideline is simply to encourage him. I don't find any passage in the Bible that says someone is wrong to pray a salvation prayer more than once. Although once is literally enough for eternity, praying more frequently might offer a child greater comfort and certainty. Especially when life gets intense.

> Don't discount a child's desire to pray for salvation on more than one occasion.

Third, consider age—but don't use age as a reason to dismiss a child's desire to start a relationship with Jesus. Psychologist Karen Maudlin says, "God honors the prayers of tender hearts time and time again. . . . It is safe to say that most children under ten have a hard time conceptualizing a 'life-long' commitment. That doesn't mean [a child's] faith is any less real."[1]

Age will, though, play a distinct role in articulating the prayer.

As much as possible, the words that the child prays should be his own—so offer only gentle guidance through the prayer's three portions. However, common sense tells us that the younger the age, the greater your expectation should be for a repeat-after-me prayer rather than for a child's ability to follow your prompt.

> Ideally, an adult explains the three components of the prayer, and then the child tells God what she admits, believes, and chooses.

The word "prompt" needs explanation. Ideally, an adult explains the three components of the prayer, and then the child tells God what she admits, believes, and chooses. But remembering all three is difficult for someone who hears about this prayer for the first time. That said, explain A and then give the child time to respond before continuing. The following serves as an example of prompting a child through the A-B-C prayer:

Okay Lisa, sounds to me like you're ready to start a relationship with Jesus. Let's pray together, and I'll help you know what to say. Here we go.

God, my friend Lisa wants to start a relationship with Jesus.

Lisa, now it's your turn to go ahead and tell God that you've done wrong stuff and ask him to forgive you ... (pause)

Good job. Now tell him that you really do believe in Jesus, and believe that he died as the punishment for the wrong stuff you've done ... (pause)

Cool. Now tell Him that you have decided to follow Jesus the rest of your life ... (pause)

Amen! Way to go Lisa!

Options on How to Respond

"Lisa" just made the most important decision of her life, one that deserves a deliberate response on your part. Consider one or all of the following four options:

1. Immediately make a big deal about the decision. Explode with words of congratulations, high fives, and any other appropriate reaction. Just avoid appearing solemn or stoic. If you're in ministry, this is what you work hard to see happen. As a parent, this is likely an incredible answer to prayer. Witnessing and participating in another person's salvation stimulates a feeling that, I believe, is as close to the euphoria of heaven as can be experienced in this world. That said, let loose with excitement.

2. Help mark the moment by giving the child something that shows the date. Send him or her a congratulations card—kids love receiving personal mail. Some people give a Bible with words of encouragement written inside the cover. I know parents who record the event in a family journal of extraordinary accomplishments. My children have their faith affirmed every time they see the exact dates of their salvations.

3. Encourage the child to continue praying. The A-B-C prayer showed them how informally they can talk with God, so remind them that relationships require people to speak to one another.

4. Ensure that the child owns a Bible he or she can read and understand. Scripture acts as God's words to us, which is a major way that he speaks as part of our relationship with him. Age plays the key role in deciding which version to purchase, and any Christian bookstore can help you.

No doubt a long list of other good ideas exists. The most important factor with any idea, though, is to give thought before it's needed so you're ready to act when a child prays. The moment will evaporate quickly if you do nothing, so pause for a moment right now and consider what you might do for your own child or one in your ministry.

The Bible directs believers to experience baptism as an outward expression of an internal decision to follow Christ. Some churches baptize people of any age who begin a relationship with Jesus, while others ask children to wait until a minimum age to assure their complete understanding. Rather than advocating one approach over another, I suggest that you follow the discernment of your church's elders. To that end, talk with kids who become Christians about baptism—whether it's an option for that day or some day in the future. Just be certain that they understand the meaning of baptism and why Christ-followers throughout the centuries have participated in this sacrament.

Next, consider the parents. If the child who prayed is your own, you have this issue covered. In children's ministries that present the salvation message during a program, though, the parents may not be present for the big moment. This gives you either a privilege or a challenge to tell those parents what happened.

The privilege will take place when the parents feel pure joy that their son or daughter is now part of God's family. The challenge will happen if the parents themselves have yet to enter into the family. In churches that deliberately reach out to unchurched people, this scenario is likely to occur. View the challenge as an opportunity.

> If you pick up any confusion when you tell a parent that his or her child began a relationship with Jesus today, then God has placed you in a new situation where eternity may be at stake.

If you pick up any confusion when you tell a parent that his or her child began a relationship with Jesus today, then God has placed you in a new situation where eternity may be at stake. Because now you have the opportunity to explain to the parent the meaning of a relationship with Jesus (see chapter 4), possibly share your own faith story (see chapter 3), and even describe how salvation begins (this chapter). You'll be surprised how preparation for these conversations with kids qualifies you to communicate clearly with adults about Jesus.

The Right Time — Any Time

Sarah Keith, a volunteer at First Presbyterian Church in North Palm Beach, Florida, knows that the right time might come at any time:

> During last night's midweek program at our church, we asked the children if the lessons we have been teaching them since they started the program have resulted in their asking Jesus to be their Savior and Forever Friend. At least five of the children raised their hands. One girl, in particular, told us she asked Jesus into her life during the salvation prayer offered following one of the games we played last year.

You never know what eternal-stakes moment you'll find yourself in, so prepare. God taught me the value of preparation one evening while I worked to prepare the original Leading Kids to Jesus training course for our children's ministry. I didn't expect a holy moment to arrive when my son, then four years old, opened the door to my office a few minutes before bedtime. But it did. In a moment as quick as a thought, the concepts I had spent hours typing on a keyboard jumped into reality.

As Scotty waited for me to turn off the computer, he spotted a century-and-a-half-old five-volume study Bible. "Where did you get those books?" he asked.

"When Great-grandpa Vander Meulen died, Grandma gave me his Bibles," I replied as we walked up the stairs to his bedroom.

"Why did Grandpa V. die?" he asked.

"Well, he lived for a long time, and just got old, I guess," I said.

Scotty pressed on, "Where did he go when he died?"

I paused and reminded myself to think—and breathe!

"Grandpa V. went to heaven," I responded.

"You mean where God and Jesus live?" Scotty countered, clearly showing he was listening in Promiseland (Willow Creek's children's ministry).

"Yes."

"Where is heaven?" was the next question he posed, and he really seemed interested to know.

"Well, where do you think it is?"

"It's way up in the sky!" was Scotty's excited response, proud to be adding facts to the conversation. "So Daddy ... how do you get to heaven?"

My pulse raced as I realized what was taking place. Then I gave it my best shot.

"You know how we say you and I are 'buddies'?" I asked. This question referred to the exclusive group the two of us had formed, promising to always be better than best friends.

"Well, to get to heaven you have to decide to be buddies with Jesus forever, which is a real long time. And part of being buddies is that you tell him you're sorry for doing wrong things, and ask him to help you do right things instead. Anyone who is buddies with Jesus gets to go to heaven. And you know what? He would love to hear you tell him you want to live with him someday in heaven."

The pause in his questions seemed to last hours, but was probably less than two seconds. "Do you think they have fire trucks to play with in heaven?"

"Well, what have you learned about God in Promiseland?" I asked.

"God can do anything!" he shouted—his enthusiastic response to that question for quite some time.

"Don't you think that if God can do anything, that he probably has the greatest fire trucks ever to play with?!" This was getting fun.

"Yeah! And Daddy, you're buddies with Jesus, right? So you're going to heaven, right?"

"Yeah, Scotty, I sure am."

"Well, do you think we can go out to breakfast all the time when we're in heaven?"

As I shut off the light and sat in his bed with him, I said, "Yeah, I'll bet we probably can." Breakfast enthusiast and bacon lover—just like his dad!

With the lights off, the time had come for prayers before drifting off to sleep. I'll never forget Scott's prayer that night.

"Excuse me God" (I've always loved his casual beginnings to prayers), "you know what? I want to always be buddies with Jesus because I want to live with you in heaven when I die. So let's always be buddies, okay? And I'm sorry when I do bad stuff, okay? And God, can you make sure you have lots of fire trucks? Thanks that I'm buddies with Jesus. Amen!"

As I sat there next to him, I wore both a smile and a tear. A very real spiritual journey was underway. As soon as I heard the familiar heavy breathing, I kissed Scott's forehead and whispered, "I love you, buddy. And I love you and thank you, Lord." As I quietly made my way out of his dark room, I still had the smile. And I had a real strong feeling that at that same moment, God had one too.

I've had a lot of thrills in life—making two free throws with four seconds left to win a double-overtime basketball game, marrying the woman of my dreams, teaching conferences full of people about leading kids to Jesus, even riding bumper cars countless times. Yet none compare with the exhilaration I felt that night with my son. And that feeling had nothing to do with what I said; it was all about what he did. Because there are some things kids must do for themselves—and the result is pure joy on earth, and a celebration in heaven.

"In the same way, I tell you, there is rejoicing in the presence of the angels of God over one sinner who repents" (Luke 15:10).

Personal Exercises

1. On the back of the note card (or on the PDA memo) you made as a personal exercise following chapter 4, write the letters A, B, and C with a short explanation of each.

2. Practice prompting a partner through an A-B-C prayer. Repeat at least twice.

CHAPTER 6

What If I Don't Have a Story?

To squeeze the most fun from your amusement park dollar, arrive before the gates open. Veteran visitors know the first hour or two offer the most fun for a simple reason—fewer people. And that means less time spent waiting in lines and more time enjoying the rides.

One summer morning, our family joined the early birds outside the main entrance of one of our favorite parks. We purchased tickets and positioned ourselves near the turnstiles, anticipating the moment we could rush inside to our favorite attractions. As we watched the clock, park workers mingled among the crowd, shouting reminders that seemed silly to me.

"Please make sure to have your ticket out."

"Everyone needs a ticket."

"Nobody gets in without a ticket."

I wondered why they felt the need to remind us of something so basic. Of course everyone would need a ticket. (Just to be safe, though, I checked to make sure I still held four of them in my possession.) The gates soon opened, and our line began to thread people single file into the park. What happened next amazed me. A young man in front of us didn't have a ticket! Instead, he handed the attendant a coupon for free admission.

"I'm sorry, sir," the ticket taker said. "First, you must have a ticket to get in. And second, the coupon is good for a free admission only when you purchase another ticket at full price."

I counted our tickets for the sixth time in less than five minutes—just to make sure I would not share this young man's embarrassment. He learned that those announcements were not so silly after all; if you go to the admission gate without a ticket, you won't get in. You can offer a coupon. You can show a credit card. You can wave a wad of one-hundred-dollar bills at the attendant. But only a purchased ticket will get you through the gate.

Picture yourself in a similar story.

You drive to an amusement park, get out of your car, and head to the admission gate. While in line, you hear that you need a ticket. So you approach the ticket window, and ask for one. The attendant tells you the price, and you gasp. Realistic story so far.

Now imagine that the amount required far surpasses all the money you'll earn in a lifetime. You stand there dumbfounded, not knowing what to do. Your only option is to get out of line. Or is it?

As you stand in the ticket line bewildered, someone calls out to you. You've heard the voice before, but this time you respond. This person wants to pay for your ticket! All you need to do is accept his generosity. In fact, he seems to be making the offer to everyone. So you finally enter the park and wonder why anyone would turn down such an opportunity.

Once inside the park, you look back toward the people who remain outside the gates. You tell several folks that they should take advantage of the free ticket offer. "It's the only way to get in, it's free," you explain, "and I did it!" The people who listen believe what you say because your words come from actual experience. They get tickets and join you inside the park.

But you also notice a few people still outside the gate, without tickets, telling others about the need for a ticket and the generous man's offer. These folks fail to convince anyone because they lack credibility. Who would follow the advice of someone who has yet to take advantage of this remarkable proposition?

An obvious analogy to accepting Jesus' free gift of grace, right? Of course it is. The "admission price" of a relationship with God surpasses anything you or I can pay, so Jesus paid it for us by dying on the cross. So how much does all this ticket talk relate to helping kids become Christians?

A lot. Because an adult can talk with kids about Jesus authentically only when he or she has a relationship with Christ. And that qualifier presents an issue for us to consider.

Research by George Barna concludes that "adults who say they are Christian but have never made a profession of faith in Jesus Christ represent almost half of all people attending Christian churches in the U.S."[1] So a large number of people who participate in church have never truly crossed the line of faith—they hang around the park entrance, but never accept the ticket to go inside.

Many of those individuals opt to volunteer. And some of them will end up in children's ministry, where discussions about faith in Jesus take place. Some may even read this book, which is why I included this chapter. This one-half of adults in church might include you. If so, relax because you've done nothing wrong; you just have more distance to travel on your spiritual journey before you recognize a personal need to accept Christ's invitation to a relationship.

That relationship could be as close as the end of this chapter. So let's get personal.

Your Ticket

In Acts 2:39, Peter describes the offer of salvation this way: "The promise is for you and your children and for all who are far off—for all whom the Lord our God will call." Notice the order—you first, then children, followed by everyone else.

How certain are you that you have a ticket? Many adults struggle with an honest answer.

Donald Cole, pastor for the Moody Broadcast Network, said the most common question asked by callers to his radio program who consider themselves Christians is "whether they can be saved and *know it*."[2] But even though wrestling with such certainty appears fairly common, keep in mind that your answer to the question carries personal, eternal implications.

In his book *The Purpose-Driven Life*, Rick Warren says, "From the Bible we can surmise that God will ask us two crucial questions: First, 'What did you do with my Son, Jesus Christ?' God won't ask about your religious background or doctrinal views. The only thing that will matter is, did you accept what Jesus did for you and did you learn to love and trust him?" Rick predicts God's second question will be equally compelling: "'What did you do with what I gave you?' What did you do with your life—all the gifts, talents, opportunities, energy, relationships, and resources God gave you?"[3]

How certain are you that you have a ticket? Many adults struggle with an honest answer.

Many people — including dedicated volunteers or seasoned church staff members — will accurately point to their ministry work in answer to God's second question. A clear, solid answer for the first question, though, will prove difficult for some of those very same folks.

So for the sake of certainty, let's double-check our tickets.

To get the most out of this chapter, try to refrain from reacting too quickly to challenges concerning your personal faith. We'll find those challenges in the context of a familiar Old Testament story. As we walk through that story, we'll consider what a relationship with God is, and just as importantly, what it is not.

SAMUEL'S STORY

In 1 Samuel, the parents of a young boy named Samuel gave him to be raised by temple officials, so he could serve God his entire life (1 Samuel 1:21–28). The lad lived and worked with a priest named Eli.

The third chapter of 1 Samuel describes a typical night at the temple—one that turned quite profound. God wanted to share important information with Samuel, but the boy did not recognize the Lord's voice.

> The boy Samuel ministered before the Lord under Eli. In those days the word of the Lord was rare; there were not many visions.
>
> One night Eli, whose eyes were becoming so weak that he could barely see, was lying down in his usual place. The lamp of God had not yet gone out, and Samuel was lying down in the temple of the Lord, where the ark of God was. Then the Lord called Samuel.

Samuel answered, "Here I am." And he ran to Eli and said, "Here I am; you called me."

But Eli said, "I did not call; go back and lie down." So he went and lay down.

Again the Lord called, "Samuel!" And Samuel got up and went to Eli and said, "Here I am; you called me."

"My son," Eli said, "I did not call; go back and lie down."

Now Samuel did not yet know the Lord: The word of the Lord had not yet been revealed to him.

The Lord called Samuel a third time, and Samuel got up and went to Eli and said, "Here I am; you called me."

Then Eli realized that the Lord was calling the boy. So Eli told Samuel, "Go and lie down, and if he calls you, say, 'Speak, Lord, for your servant is listening.'" So Samuel went and lay down in his place.

The Lord came and stood there, calling as at the other times, "Samuel! Samuel!"

Then Samuel said, "Speak, for your servant is listening."

And the Lord said to Samuel: "See, I am about to do something in Israel that will make the ears of everyone who hears of it tingle."

1 Samuel 3:1–11

Notice a key statement tucked midway through the narrative of God's repeated calls: "Now Samuel did not yet know the Lord" (verse 7). In other words, Samuel had yet to begin a significant relationship with God.

The phrase "begin a significant relationship with God" deserves clarification for this story to make sense. Many people lack this clarity and don't even realize it—I have firsthand experience.

At twenty-nine, I learned the important difference between knowing information about God and knowing that I have a relationship with Christ. I believed sin was wrong, but I needed to believe that *my* sins were wrong. I believed Christ died on the cross, but I needed to believe that he died for *me*. I believed he offers forgiveness for sins to all people, but I had to believe that *I* needed that forgiveness. All my knowledge about God became personal belief—a conviction so strong that it compelled me to accept Jesus' gift of grace, and then commit the rest of my life to an active relationship with him.

Even though Samuel devoted his life to ministry (verse 1: "The boy Samuel ministered before the Lord")—he did not yet know the Lord. Although to some people this might seem incredible or impossible, that still happens today among church staff members or key volunteers.

The first time I taught the Leading Kids to Jesus workshop at the Willow Creek Promiseland conference, a woman approached me as I stepped offstage. She told me that one of her ministry colleagues had left the room in tears. According to this woman, her friend realized that she had never truly started a relationship with Jesus. That realization upset her because she had already served in ministry for a number of years. "What should I do?" her friend asked.

> At twenty-nine, I learned the important difference between knowing information about God and knowing that I have a relationship with Christ.

"Help your friend pray the A-B-C prayer [as explained in chapter 5]," I replied, "and then celebrate!" And they did. I've been gratified to witness that same scenario many times through the years, as I've taught the workshop in locations around the world.

Let's look again at Samuel. He lived life surrounded by God's people and close to God's word. Verse 3 says, "Samuel was lying down in the temple of the Lord, where the ark of God was." Verse 9 refers to Samuel's sleeping spot as "his place."

Samuel spent so much time in the temple that he became a regular fixture. And despite living much of his life surrounded by and participating in religious activities—where others most likely viewed him as a dedicated servant—Samuel did not yet know the Lord. That still happens today with people who actively attend church for years.

For five years I volunteered in our church's evangelism ministry. Among its many responsibilities, our team read the written testimonies of all adults registered for baptism. What a privilege! We frequently pored over stories from individuals who attended church for years and often served as ministry volunteers. Inevitably, each story described a life-changing moment that brought clarity and awareness about that person's need for a savior. Everybody's journey to faith took different turns, but each one ended in a similar place—Admitting sins, Believing Christ died for those sins, and Choosing to follow him (not coincidentally, the components of the A-B-C prayer!). These stories confirmed that church involvement sometimes precedes a personal relationship with Jesus. And that's fine—as long as the relationship eventually gets underway.

God's Nudging

Despite God's ability to communicate with people in countless ways, he chose to nudge a young boy and wait for a response, even before that individual knew the Lord. Today, God still nudges people who do not yet know him. And he still waits for a response.

Is it possible that throughout chapter 3, while we focused on writing and refining your story of faith, you realized you don't have one? In chapter 4 did the salvation plan—worded for kids—make sense to you in ways that it never has before? Or in chapter 5 did you read about a prayer that you have yet to say?

If your heart whispered yes to any of these questions, then maybe God has nudged you. And maybe that prompt will point you to an honest realization that you still need to take faith's ultimate step—"confess with your mouth, 'Jesus is Lord,' and believe in your heart that God raised him from the dead"

(Romans 10:9). While your answer may be forming, I repeat my request that you resist any reaction or firm conclusion for just a bit longer.

The purpose of this book is to help people talk clearly with kids about Jesus. So with that same spirit, let's put words to truths that offer clarity about Christianity to adults. Although Christians go to Sunday services, attending church or other religious activities does not make someone a Christian. Although many Christians invest their time and talents serving God, volunteering at church does not make someone a Christian. Nor does knowing the Bible well. Or even being a really good person.

> Today, God still nudges people who do not yet know him. And he still waits for a response.

Samuel did all that and did not yet know the Lord. In similar fashion, C. S. Lewis once described a key point in his journey toward authentic faith: "I have just passed on from believing in God to definitely believing in Christ—in Christianity."[4]

Personal Question 1—What Would Jesus Say? What about you? The predictable question is to ask if you have a relationship with Christ. But a more striking question to ponder is this: Would *Jesus* say that you are in a relationship with him? He testifies to the importance of your answer in Matthew 7:23: "Then I will tell them plainly, 'I never knew you. Away from me.'" Good-intentioned people will seek to enter heaven based on their knowledge of Christ—or maybe based on work done at church—only to be turned away because Christ did not truly know them. So what would Jesus say right now about you? Take a break from reading to let your heart dance with that question for a while.

During a recent breakfast meeting, my friend Dave served up a summary of his spiritual journey: "I knew a lot of verses while growing up. But my life didn't change until I figured out that God isn't just on the pages of the Bible; he is beside me." And that change of location—from printed page to personal presence—makes a world of difference because it begs a response.

Eli tells Samuel that the voice he keeps hearing is God's (1 Samuel 3:9), and instructs Samuel to respond directly to the Almighty by answering: "Speak, Lord, for your servant is listening." Samuel decides to follow Eli's advice. The Lord honors this clear response, and tells Samuel about events that will soon take place—a conversation that begins a lifelong dialogue between God and this new young prophet. To Samuel, God no longer existed merely on the scrolls of Scripture.

Personal Question 2—Have You Responded? Shane Claiborne, a street missionary in Philadelphia who is also a compelling speaker, offers a challenging perspective on Jesus' words in the Bible by asking: "What if he really meant this stuff?"[5] Assuming that Jesus was serious about what he said, your life and mine ought to show evidence of his words' impact. Has that happened? Take a moment right now and whisper, "Speak, Lord, for I am listening." Then read these words from Jesus, and let yourself wonder about the impact they should make on your life:

> *"I am the way and the truth and the life. No one comes to the Father except through me."*
>
> *John 14:6*

> *"Seek first his kingdom and his righteousness."*
>
> *Matthew 6:33*

> *"I have come that they may have life, and have it to the full."*
>
> *John 10:10*

> *"I have told you this so that my joy may be in you and that your joy may be complete."*
>
> *John 15:11*

" 'Love the Lord your God with all your heart and with all your soul and with all your mind.' This is the first and greatest commandment."

Matthew 22:37–38

"Come, follow me."

Luke 18:22

To authentically lead a child into a relationship with Christ requires you to be in one first. You can only give away that which you have. And if something inside you has started to stir, pause from reading right now and respond to God. As you learned in chapter 5, it's as easy as A-B-C (Admit, Believe, Choose).

Still Holding Out?

For some people, the hardest part of becoming a Christian is to escape from underneath their own pride, and to humbly tell Christ they want to start a relationship with him. If you're a church volunteer or employee, then pulling back that pride can be even tougher—the expectation exists, after all, that

Admit your sins
Believe in Jesus
Choose to follow Jesus

you have Christianity figured out. If this is the case with you, please relax. People figure out the need for Jesus at different paces and at different times in life. And sometimes that time comes as a surprise.

Legendary basketball coach John Wooden once said, "When I was baptized, I really hadn't accepted Christ. I thought I had, but I hadn't."[6] Coach Wooden is but one of many people who understand a truth articulated by Rick Warren in *The Purpose-Driven Life*: "Baptism doesn't make you a member of God's family, only faith in Christ does that."[7]

That same, sometimes surprising, truth applies to other ceremonies or rituals as well. In the Bible, God says our hearts are what he desires most: "To love him with all your heart, with all your understanding and with all your strength, and to love your neighbor as yourself is more important than all burnt offerings and sacrifices" (Mark 12:33).

Good news awaits when you arrive at the realization that you need to respond: God won't be surprised! He's expecting you. He's waited your whole life for you to come to him. That wait has been shorter for some people than for others, which actually can introduce its own unique challenge.

Statistics show that most Christians began their relationship with Jesus by age thirteen.[8] And at that age, "What did I have to repent from? Hitting my sister?" asks former Moody Bible Institute president Joe Stowell in reference to his childhood salvation.[9] Because the life change resulting from a childhood commitment may have been less than dramatic, the memory of that decision might prove difficult to recall many years later. That's okay. Remember that Scripture tells us that kids can start a relationship with Jesus—the passionate belief that serves as this book's foundation!

If you have a cloudy memory of your childhood decision to become a Christian, spend a few moments considering modified versions of this chapter's two personal questions. First, what would Jesus list as specific differences your faith

> Because the life change resulting from a childhood commitment may have been less than dramatic, the memory of that decision might prove difficult to recall many years later. That's okay.

in him has made throughout various time periods in your life? Second, what choices do you make today as a result of your belief as a Christ-follower? *When* you made the decision to follow Jesus matters little compared with what you do *now* with that faith.

And finally, let's acknowledge one last challenge that can sometimes create confusion. Many people, like Samuel, initially misinterpret God's call to them. Some take it as a directive to try hard to be a good person—one who doesn't lie, cheat, steal, or curse—and they spend life frustrated with their failures. Or they might reason that the good they do outweighs the bad, and hope that God knows how to calculate an average. Some believe God wants them to perform well on a divine grading curve—they only need to score better than most people. Others feel they've answered the Lord's call when they acquiesce to a spouse's, parent's, or friend's wishes to clean up their lives. C. S. Lewis once said, "We must not suppose that even if we succeeded in making everyone nice we should have saved their souls. A world of nice people, content in their own niceness, looking no further, turned away from God, would be just as desperately in need of salvation as a miserable world—and might even be more difficult to save."[10] Still others believe that God calls them to obey a multitude of rules, doctrines, and dogma that religious life expects—or possibly requires. That belief, shared by way too many people, creates spiritual busyness that unfortunately drives many people away from God.

These misinterpretations—being really good, being relatively good, behaving for those watching, or immersing oneself in rigid religion—miss the mark because they involve judgment by other people. Complication constantly arises from human expectations for how you and I should live because we can never be good enough by these standards. God offers a simpler plan.

The Lord spoke to Samuel at night in private. Had the conversation taken place in the presence of Eli, the prophet likely would have confirmed God's voice for Samuel—he might have even responded to God instead of trusting the boy to talk with the Almighty. But Samuel learned that God wanted to relate with him on a *personal* level—one that involved no one else. In similar fashion, God desires that you and I relate directly with him. Other people's wishes, desires, and directives are superfluous. What matters is that you and I can honestly say, "I'm a Christian because I'm in a relationship with Christ." That's all that counts.

MOVING INTO A TRUE RELATIONSHIP WITH CHRIST

For a year shy of three decades, I labeled myself a Christian for a variety of reasons other than the right one. My family attended a Christian church, and I became a member. I lived in the United States, which is a Christian country, right? I even owned a Bible and knew several of its stories.

Had I sat through training or read a book on how to lead kids to Jesus, I might even have come up with a story of how I became a Christian—not with any ill intent, just out of confusion and a lack of understanding the truth about a relationship with Jesus. A feeling of discomfort undoubtedly would have accompanied that story, though, because it would have lacked authenticity. Fortunately, I eventually moved away from such self-deception and into a true relationship with Christ.

Now that you've finished reading this chapter, I pray that you are confident in what Jesus would say about you, based on your response to him. With that faith, you can feel great about your story—whether it involves events from years past, or just the last twenty minutes. Regardless of when it happened, you have an authentic story to tell about how you came to possess life's most valuable ticket.

Personal Exercise

Write a letter to Jesus that describes the relationship you and he share, and the difference he has made in your life. If this exercise seems at all difficult, review the four-part gospel outline in chapter 4, and then reread this chapter.

CHAPTER 7

The Early Years

'll always remember the first ride my son and I took in the Space Shuttle. Not a real shuttle—an amusement park virtual reality attraction that captured his three-year-old imagination. Even to a thirty-three-year-old it looked real.

Our cruise of the cosmos aboard this full-scale replica of a NASA shuttle actually began as we stood in line. The detailed decor and believable background noises convinced us that we had stepped into an actual rocket launch center. Prior to the shuttle doors opening, flight control personnel briefed Scott, me, and the staging room filled with fellow astronauts about what to expect on our journey—just like they do at NASA, or so I imagined. After settling into our seats, the multiscreen video and audio experience—complete with choreographed seat jolts and vibrations—delivered a thrilling trip to space and back. So realistic that, despite constant self-reminders that this was merely a movie and simulated experience, a twinge of very real motion sickness hit me. As the shuttle glided through a perfect virtual landing, my excitement returned—this time to get off the ride.

As Scott and I walked away from the faux ship, the fresh air helped me regain my equilibrium. Within a few yards, though,

Scott suggested that we stop. Turning back toward the shuttle, we watched the next group of space travelers board. We continued to watch as more people got in line. And we kept watching, with Scott's eyes glued on the flying machine that towered in front of us.

"Scotty, do you want to ride it again?" I asked, trying to ignore the queasiness that question prompted.

"No, not really," he responded. We watched awhile longer.

"Buddy, if we're not going to ride it again, why are we standing here?" I asked.

His reason provided me with a memorable line that still makes me smile: "I want to see it take off!"

He thought that the shuttle replica would fire its main engines and blast out of the park. To Scott the experience had seemed real. All the adults who operated the ride gave instructions for a journey into space, so why wouldn't he believe them?

BELIEF WITHOUT QUESTIONING

That moment illustrated a key truth that Karyn Henley describes in *Child-Sensitive Teaching*: "Young children generally believe what they are told without questioning whether it is true."[1] Fortunately, in the case of Christianity, we have a message based entirely on truth.

In *Teaching Kids about God*, John Trent (et al.) offers a similar thought. "Between birth and kindergarten," he writes, "kids are ultimately receptive."[2] Can you see the ministry potential presented by receptivity?

Clearly, these early years offer an era of opportunity for adults to lay a spiritual foundation in youngsters that will someday support a strong faith. The potential payoff of influencing children during this season of life forms the rationale behind Francis Xavier's comment, "Give me kids until they're seven, and then anyone can have them."[3] And an unexpected conversation with my daughter demonstrated to me the wisdom behind that statement.

Two-year-old Erin loved her dolls. One day, she and I spent an afternoon on the floor of her room with her complete doll family. I was entrusted with the daddy figure, and performed as best as I could. She capably took responsibility for the mommy, sister, brother, grandma, grandpa, and two neighbors.

As I tried to stay focused on the pretend world I found myself in, she surprised me with a question: "Daddy, you *lub* Jesus?"

Shocked, I replied, "Of course I do, sweetie."

She proceeded to ask if Mommy (her real one) and brother Scott loved Jesus too. "Sure do," I responded in both cases. Satisfied with the answers, she went back into the doll family fantasy neighborhood.

But eager to stretch this moment out further, I asked her, "Erin, do *you* love Jesus?" and held my breath.

To my surprise—and joy—she said in a cool and casual manner, "Yeah, I *lub* Jesus."

Although this episode took place prior to God placing me in children's ministry, as a parent I had a good idea about what prompted our conversation. I'm convinced Erin heard about loving Jesus and how Jesus loves her from someone in Promiseland, and that caused her to decide that she too would "lub Jesus."

These early years offer an era of opportunity for adults to lay a spiritual foundation in youngsters that will someday support a strong faith.

An adult volunteer—someone filled with conviction that two-year-olds need God—probably said within the three seconds of my daughter's attention span that he or she loved Jesus. And because of the way it stuck with Erin, chances are strong that this was someone who picked my little girl up when she cried, played games with her on the floor, and spent time talking with her.

A big revelation took place that day in my daughter's room: Erin and Jesus had started to form a relationship. At least they had according to what she believed—a belief so strong that she wanted to be sure her mommy, daddy, and brother shared it. A belief so real that she would think it odd for anyone to suggest otherwise. From that point on, the world would have a far more difficult time trying to convince my daughter that a relationship with Jesus is wrong or impossible. Sorry, world. I've been told her stubbornness comes from my side, which for once I'll claim as a compliment. Five years later, her beliefs remain strong—as shown by her words that appeared in a portion of chapter 2 called the Gospel According to Erin.

BELIEF WITHOUT COMPLETE UNDERSTANDING

Of course a world of difference exists between believing something is true and understanding every aspect of it. Yet while God expects us to believe, he never commands his people to have complete understanding. Many of the Bible's faith-filled servants provide us with great examples of this principle. Noah did not understand about the storm front just over the horizon, but he did believe that God wanted him to build a boat. Moses had no idea how a bush could burn and not turn into ashes, but he believed God spoke to him through it. The blind man in John 9 believed in the power of Jesus to heal him, but had no idea how it could possibly happen. Without hesitation, he boldly walked before the powerful religious officials and stated the only thing that mattered to him: "One thing I do know. I was blind but now I see!"

> A two-year-old *can* extend a little piece of her heart to Jesus — a truth that transforms the floor of every church's preschool room into an evangelism field.

(verse 25). Belief at any age serves as a strong step toward faith.

Did Erin experience salvation at two? No. At two years old, she did not understand all of what becoming a Christian means. Years later she would become a forever friend with Christ when she sincerely said the A-B-C prayer (discussed in chapter 5). But a two-year-old *can* extend a little piece of her heart to Jesus—a truth that transforms the floor of every church's preschool room into an evangelism field. John Trent (et al.) acknowledges such an opportunity when he says, "It's never too early for God's created people to do the very thing he created them for: have a deep friendship with him."[4] And to that end, the rest of the chapter will examine three areas of focus for deliberate, effective ministry to children in their early years.

How to Effectively Reach a Young Child

Positively Connect the Child's World to God

Acts 17 tells the story of the apostle Paul's encounter with the people of Athens, including his persuasive words to help them understand God (verses 16–32). Perhaps you've never thought of that scriptural passage from this perspective, but I suggest mimicking his approach in reaching out to children. Specifically, Paul noticed that Athens was a city full of worship idols— including an altar "to an unknown god." The apostle proceeded to connect the world of the Athenians to the true God, when he said, "What you worship as something unknown I am going to proclaim to you" (verse 23). From Paul's example we learn that creating a connection between a person's surroundings and the Lord can serve as a strong starting point to reach someone to whom God seems unknown. Such as young kids.

The rest of Paul's speech in Acts 17 appeals to religious people and philosophers, so let's take his lead as we build an appropriate approach to use with children. That approach begins with understanding an important, basic requirement that precedes any relationship with God; a person must have awareness of God. In Romans 10:14 (NRSV), Paul describes the importance of this concept and the inherent responsibility it places on believers: "But how are they to call on one in whom they have not believed? And how are they to believe in one of whom they have never heard? And how are they to hear without someone to proclaim him?"

Proclaim the Lord to young kids? Paul's words lay out a challenge that may seem most unattainable for workers in the infants' room, because they may believe that the littlest of kids lack the ability to comprehend God. That perception needs to change faster than a six-hour-old diaper!

In *Child-Sensitive Teaching*, Karyn Henley describes the importance of introducing babies to God in very simple ways. To do this, she says, we must create an association between kids' sensory experiences and God.[5] The result can be a strong connection between their world and the one who created the world, even when they don't yet know the meanings of words used.

Making connection points is simple. As an infant experiences joy, rest, peace, warmth, or wonder, then talk to that child with clear emphasis on God's role in what's taking place.

For instance, while providing comfort to a fussy child, softly tell her, "I'm here for you, and God is always here for you." Karyn Henley suggests telling a baby enjoying a banana, "God made this banana."[6] And while spending time holding a little one in a rocking chair, sing songs to him that clearly and frequently use the names God and Jesus. If, like me, you have the vocal talent of an injured farm animal, then remember to sing softly. And smile.

Over time, little minds will remember the name of the Almighty and the feeling experienced as they heard that name. An automatic, internal connection between God and a warm hug, tasty snack, soothing voice, and bright eyes gives kids a giant head start toward a future friendship with the Lord. Let's discard the words "I *just* take care of the babies" and replace them with "I introduce babies to God!"

Just ask author and pastor Jack Hayford at The Church on the Way in Los Angeles, California. In his book *Blessing Your Children*, he says, "We train even the nursery workers to recognize the power of their personal touch on the babies in their care. Those who are part of that ministry are trained to believe in and exercise spiritual vitality and love in a way that can impart life to their young charges. By prayer, singing, and speaking tender words—even sitting and rocking an infant—an infusion of the life of the Holy Spirit can flow from these workers into that baby."[7]

Clearly Communicate God's Truth and Love

At some point in every adult's life, you and I inherit the habit of complicating everything. We may discard a belief that God said, "Let there be light; and there was light," in favor of speculation about a big bang. Rainbows become a refracted spectrum illuminated from airborne water molecules instead of an artistic reminder of a divine promise. And the thought of avoiding leaf-raking duties by cutting down that big maple in the backyard replaces the wonder that God creates beautiful trees. Young kids need for us to reject this unfortunate inheritance.

As children move out of the infant stage and into ages two and three, a new opportunity emerges to usher them closer to God: to verbally communicate God's truth and love in tiny, bite-sized pieces. The recipe for success includes common and uncomplicated ingredients that all of us possess—simple thoughts, plain words, and short sentences.

In similar fashion to "God made this banana," adults can declare truths about God to little ones in terms of the world the child sees or experiences. Dr. James Dobson says, "Even at three years of age, a child is capable of learning that the flowers, the sky, the birds and even the rainbow are gifts from God's hand."[8] With their fresh capability to learn, kids eagerly soak up explanations about a world they long to understand. Let's look at a practical example.

The team in our ministry's three-year-old area taught a summer unit titled "God made the world." A rather big concept for sure, so each week we examined a piece of God's creation that someone aged three could readily understand. The week I served as a small group leader, we featured the topic "God created the animals."

> The recipe for success includes common and uncomplicated ingredients that all of us possess — simple thoughts, plain words, and short sentences.

The large group lesson explained in very simple words that God created animals in Genesis 1, followed by a pretend trip through the zoo where we repeated the words of truth, "God made the animals." Then small group time began.

As we munched a snack — animal crackers, of course — we took turns saying the name of an animal, and then stating that God made that creature. I added the fun twist of letting each child act like the animal he or she named. For example, on my turn I got on my hands and knees and growled real loud. After someone correctly guessed "a bear," we all said together, "God made the bears!" As it turned out, our group had lots of bears.

After going around the circle twice, the group had learned the lesson cold, but the parents had not yet come from big church to pick up their kids. With a few extra minutes at my disposal, I showed the group — to their amazement — that I could balance an empty paper cup (it previously held my crackers) on my head. No, the lesson plan did not include the cup trick; extra fun was its only purpose. As the parents started to come into the room, I quickly took the cup off my head and passed out the take-home sheets.

When Julio's father approached the group, Julio stood up with a huge smile on his face and said, "Dad, guess what I learned today!" At the same time, he started to raise his paper cup. "Oh no, Julio," I thought, "don't put your cup on your head!"

But then, to my relief, Julio stated loudly and proudly, "God made the animals!" Yes, he remembered the right thing from our time together.

I watched a little boy walk away who believed he had figured out a piece of this world because he knew who made the animals—God. This lesson worked with Julio because it communicated a simple truth using plain words in a short sentence. And it teaches us adults the value of deliberately choosing words and looking for opportunities to share them.

What length is short enough? Years of experience in our ministry show four words or less to be an effective guideline. Sentences limited to that length can efficiently communicate God's truth and love, with increased odds that a child will remember the words and have the ability to say them on his or her own.

Consider several four-word statements of God's truth that a two- or three-year-old will understand:

- God made the animals.
- God made the sky.
- God will help me.
- The Bible is true.

The list could go on for many pages. To simplify the application of this tool, look around the environment in which you encounter kids. Based on these surroundings, make a list of several potential four-word sentences you can try immediately. Toys or stuffed animals, picture books, the view out a window—all can prompt opportunities. Speaking these words with kids will turn what might seem as idle playtime into ideal moments to offer insight about God.

Be sure to include statements about love on your list. You will share an incredible gift with young kids when they hear you, an adult they interact with and trust, talk about *your* love for Jesus and Jesus' love for you. Just remember to keep it simple and short so that a child can repeat the words if they choose to: "Jesus loves me," "Jesus loves you," and "I *lub* Jesus." What an incredible opportunity we have to give kids the most important words in life before doubt, skepticism, or complications ever exist!

Actively Reinforce the Message

Apart from any spoken words, actions also play key roles in communicating about God. Imagine the love expressed when you pick up a crying child to provide comfort—measured by how that act makes her feel. In *Teaching Kids about God*, John Trent (et al.) says, "As you hold them, love them, feed them, and keep them warm, you establish that their world is good and safe. In time, as you tell them that God loves them and looks after them, they make the connection between your loving behaviors and God's active love for them."[9] Those behaviors begin with newborns and need to continue as kids grow. And what started in a rocking chair can expand to actions that will take ministry workers to their knees. Literally.

Prior to working on this chapter today, I spent the morning in our ministry's early childhood area. An interesting sight unfolded before me in the four- and five-year-old room, courtesy of several adult volunteers. Mr. Andrew sat on the floor with a boy to read him a book. Ms. Laurie balanced on one knee as she helped three girls color pictures. On hands and knees, Mr. Jeff talked about and imitated dinosaurs with an enthusiastic handful of kids. Ms. Stephanie knelt by a small table to help children write their names on colored tags. At fifteen minutes before the start of our church service, every adult was on the ground in some position ministering to kids—and loving it!

How does time on the floor qualify as ministry? Easy. When a child sees a really big person (all adults are really big to kids!) come down to his level, that kid feels a sense of value. The thought "I must be important" goes through his mind. And if that child believes he has value in the eyes of big people, the child moves closer to a belief that God values him. The leap to "God loves me" becomes an easier step to take.

And kids aren't the only ones touched from such interactions. Fred Van Iten, a retired high school golf coach who oversees a portion of our early childhood area, says, "There's nothing like the chance to tell a two-year-old about God." Many times that chance happens on one knee or on all fours. It might even involve an appropriate hug or high five. Jesus taught extensively on this concept, and he did it without the need for words.

Jesus put his hands on children to bless them. "Then little children were being brought to him in order that he might lay his hands on them and pray. The disciples spoke sternly to those who brought them; but Jesus said, 'Let the little children come to me, and do not stop them; for it is to such as these that the kingdom of heaven belongs.' And he laid his hands on them and went on his way" (Matthew 19:13–15 NRSV). He could have simply stood and prayed in the direction of the kids, but he knew the power of touch to communicate with children.

Or imagine the love that lepers felt when Jesus physically touched them. These afflicted people, considered unclean and unhealthy by the rest of society, likely had no other person come even close to them. But Christ knew the potential to communicate a divine love through touch. The contact may have been brief with some, but the power of those moments changed people—probably even those who watched. The impact of Jesus' willingness to make contact with lepers receives an underscore when Matthew begins his numerous descriptions of Christ's miracles with the account of a cleansed leper (see Matthew 8:1–4).

I witnessed the power of touch in a volunteer role that involved helping a wheelchair-confined boy participate in our ministry despite physical challenges. One Sunday morning, as we said our goodbyes, he looked like he wanted me to hug him. I had never hugged him to that point, and didn't know how. I feared I might somehow hurt him. But I bent over anyhow, reached my hands around him as best as I could, and hugged him. He hugged me tight and for a long time. Finally, with my back starting to hurt, I stood up. "That was some hug!" I said.

He replied, "Not many people want to hug me."

Time for another confession: Hugging is an act outside my comfort zone when it involves anyone other than my wife and our two kids. But I still feel an uncomfortable lump in my throat when I consider that too many Sundays passed by before I gave that young boy a hug around his shoulders. When I consider the impact of that instant, I challenge myself to broaden my comfort zone. I must avoid any assumption that kids feel God's love elsewhere in life, and I urge you to do the same.

The topic of nonverbal communication goes beyond comforting crying kids, playing with them on the floor, or extending arms for an appropriate hug or high five. Speaking without words seems simple in the early years, but it increases in complexity as kids grow. For that reason, this chapter focuses on appropriate initiatives within the context of young children, while the next chapter takes an in-depth look at this subject for older kids.

When we positively connect a child's world to God, clearly communicate God's truth and love, and actively reinforce the message, we play a key role in leading kids to Jesus. And we do so with the understanding that sometimes steps along the way are large and sometimes they're small. But regardless of the stride length or footprint size, every step is important. Because when we share God's truth and love, we pave the way for future spiritual development. Peter writes of the desire to see people "grow up in ... salvation" once they "have tasted that the Lord is good" (1 Peter 2:2). We *can* give kids in their early years a little taste—one that will grow into a real hunger in the not-so-distant future.

Personal Exercises

1. List several simple, four-word statements in each of the following categories:

   • Who God is_____

   • What God does _____

   • Things we see that remind us of God_____

   • Descriptions of God's love _____

2. Write a note of affirmation to each volunteer or co-worker in your early childhood area about the important role he or she plays in a child's spiritual development.

CHAPTER 8

Big Discussions Happen in Small Groups

Thrill ride operators work hard to ensure the safety of all riders by examining every person's seat belt or iron restraining bar. At amusement park entrances, ticket takers move thousands of people through the turnstiles—a task they accomplish one person and one ticket at a time. Even the refreshment stand workers have a target daily volume of ice cream to sell, which they reach by dispensing one expensive cone after another. These people face a clear challenge—to provide effective, personal attention to individuals while also serving a larger group. Children's ministry must do the same.

While this book focuses on the importance of one-to-one interactions with kids, these conversations often take place, or at least begin, within the context of a group. This setting presents a twofold challenge: First, you must effectively connect with individuals. Second, those singular connections must take place while several sets of eyes look to you for leadership and direction. Leaders operate within the reality that their actions, including the manner in which they model Christian life, play a significant role in both the individual child's and the overall group's spiritual journey.

Rick Warren begins one chapter of *The Purpose-Driven Life* with the words, "You are called to belong, not just believe."[1] That truth doesn't exclusively apply to adults. We can and should offer each of the kids in our ministries an opportunity to belong—to be part of a group. Your call is to make the most of this important opportunity.

This chapter offers a core belief and four sets of personal skills that can positively impact how you lead a group of children—as a small group leader, Sunday school teacher, Christian educator, midweek program volunteer, or in any other ministry role in which you regularly meet with the same kids. To be succinct, I'll refer to you as a "group leader" for the rest of this chapter. And even if your ministry assignment does not involve groups, we'll explore various ways you can better interact with the kids you serve.

THE BELIEF

One response that came up during research for this chapter struck me as profound by virtue of its simplicity: To lead a great group you just need to be a great group leader. Likewise, this thought will point you down the path to that end: *You can be a great group leader if you believe that Jesus is present in your group, and allow that truth to guide your actions.*

That's quite a lofty belief. But it's realistic when you consider that in Matthew 18:20 Jesus said, "For where two or three come together in my name, there am I with them." Consider for a moment how you might change the way you lead a group if you believe that Jesus sits among your kids. Imagine how deliberate you would become to make every moment count. Your awareness of Jesus' presence would serve as a powerful reminder of what ministry strives to accomplish.

Embrace the conviction that as a group leader your deliberate actions will help kids walk closer to Christ. The Bible says that the behaviors, attitudes, and practices of Christians count plenty in introducing people to Jesus. For example, in Acts 16 a Roman jailer became a follower after he observed how Paul and Silas conducted themselves. What did the jailer see? Two men filled with faith, jailed for it, passionate enough about it to worship God in the middle of prison, and living out this faith in their actions.

> You can be a great group leader if you believe that Jesus is present in your group, and allow that truth to guide your actions.

After they had been severely flogged, they were thrown into prison, and the jailer was commanded to guard them carefully. Upon receiving such orders, he put them in the inner cell and fastened their feet in the stocks.

About midnight Paul and Silas were praying and singing hymns to God, and the other prisoners were listening to them. Suddenly there was such a violent earthquake that the foundations of the prison were shaken. At once all the prison doors flew open, and everybody's chains came loose. The jailer woke up, and when he saw the prison doors open, he drew his sword and was about to kill himself because he thought the prisoners had escaped. But Paul shouted, "Don't harm yourself! We are all here!"

The jailer called for lights, rushed in and fell trembling before Paul and Silas. He then brought them out and asked, "Sirs, what must I do to be saved?"

They replied, "Believe in the Lord Jesus, and you will be saved—you and your household."

Acts 16:23–33

The trust-filled choice Paul and Silas made—to serve the jailer by remaining under his guard despite the opportunity for easy freedom—was an act that brought him to Jesus.

Impacting people for Christ through your actions is far from simple. Fortunately, no matter how rough your ministry setting, you aren't in chains and sitting in a Roman jail—and I assume you've suffered no floggings. But you will face the challenge to do your best every Sunday morning because young people focus on you—similar to those watching Paul and Silas and with the same stakes at hand. Although Jesus possesses the ability, he probably won't rock the Richter scale this weekend to form a relationship with every kid you lead, just like he did for the jailer. But he could. We can, though, increase our proficiency in skill areas that will improve our impact as group leaders. And we should. Great leaders feel a rumble of urgency to do their best when they understand that they have only a brief season of kids' lives in which to make a difference.

FOUR SEASONS

For the past several summers, I've gone to a father-son camp with my son. One year we traveled there in July—always the hottest month in our area of the country. We learned, however, that the calendar offers no guarantees about the weather.

The second day of camp we woke to a typical summer day. The sun shone bright. The crisp night air had yielded to warmth. A mosquito flew around my ear, looking for a tasty site to strike. Scott and I bounced out of bed and went to breakfast.

During our meal, the sky turned gray, the wind picked up, and the temperature dropped. Another father remarked that in the time it took to eat a pancake, autumn arrived.

As we walked back to our cabin, the rain began. By the time we were safely inside, the temperature had dropped even further and the rain had turned to hail. We could see our breath in the air, and we were convinced winter was upon us.

When we saw that the ground was covered with the tiny white pellets, we did what only makes sense to dads and sons—we went outside. Sure, the ice stung a little, but it was fun to pack into balls and throw at each other. Besides, no moms were around to tell us we had to stay inside.

Thirty minutes later the sun emerged from behind the dark clouds, and the sky cleared. The temperature began to rise, the hail melted, and spring arrived.

By noon, the temperature rose to normal for July and summer returned. In just a short period of time, we had experienced all four seasons.

FOUR SEASONS, FOUR SKILL SETS

Group meetings also take place in a short span of time, and leading those meetings effectively requires several skills. All these personal techniques conveniently segment into categories that we can equate to the four seasons. If you can remember all the seasons, you can remember these skills. Just prepare to incorporate each of them into every meeting.

Spring: Growth

A key word to associate with this season is *growth*. Plants grow during the spring, and to facilitate that process, gardeners plant seeds, water frequently, and fertilize. In similar fashion, great group leaders nurture kids' spiritual growth when they deliberately say the right words. And the skillful use of three types of words deserves particular attention.

1. *Make statements that plant seeds of spiritual truth.* Curriculum plays a key role in prompting a leader through key concepts to share with kids, but don't rely on the lesson plan for

all your words. Before your group meets, spend time thinking through the words you will use to describe an attribute of God that might arise during discussion. A clear and smooth explanation of God's attitude toward sin delivers considerably more impact in the mind of a child than disjointed thoughts peppered with "ums" and "uhs." As covered in chapter 3, always be prepared to offer a description of how you became a Christian ("Always be prepared to give an answer to everyone who asks you to give the reason for the hope that you have," 1 Peter 3:15). Even leading prayer time, when done well, is a valuable skill. As I've mentioned, using words kids understand serves as the key to success.

2. *Ask open-ended questions that will challenge a child to mentally picture how to apply God's truth to his or her life.* The likelihood of spiritual growth increases when you ask questions that require more than yes or no answers. The goal is for critical thought to take place.

For example, answering the question "Do you think God hears your prayers?" takes a split second and minimal mental engagement. On the other hand, a question such as "When God listens to us pray, what do you think he might want us to say?" will provoke thought—and might just plant a spiritual seed that will sprout the next time a child prays.

3. *Offer words of affirmation to make a child feel valued.* That boy or girl might never hear those words, except from you. By the time kids arrive in your group, they've likely faced some tough struggles with self-esteem during the previous week. In fact, in her book *What Kids Really Want That Money Can't Buy*, author Betsy Taylor references a study showing that 100 percent of kids experience being called hurtful names by other kids at school. Another statistic Taylor cites further supports the need for your affirmation: "From a kid's perspective, being popular means you are okay. To be ignored or rejected means you're nobody. According to research at

> By the time kids arrive in your group, they've likely faced some tough struggles with self-esteem during the previous week.

Duke University, only 15 percent of kids are considered popular in any given school."[2]

Consider these realities while you think about how much the simplest affirming words will mean to a child. Great group leaders catch kids doing something right and offer specific encouragement. And they know that the only way to notice is to constantly look. Imagine the impact of saying, "The way you smile when you talk with your friends shows me that you have a big heart that enjoys people." In addition to what you observe, ask about a child's hobbies, sports interests, and other activities to cue you for the words to say that will build up that particular child's self-worth.

Season	Key word	Skills/actions
Spring	Growth	Make statements that plant seeds of spiritual truth. Ask open-ended questions. Offer words of affirmation.

Summer: Fun

The key word to consider for this season is *fun*. Children willingly participate in and return to activities they believe to be fun. That includes group meetings, and three specific skills will equip you to lead a group that kids look forward to.

1. *As a small group leader, fun starts when you exhibit a good attitude.* How will they notice? Because of a smile! Children know whether or not you want to be there, and that will influence their own enthusiasm about attending. Proverbs 15:13 (MSG) says, "A cheerful heart brings a smile to your face." And a smile on a leader's face will bring cheer to a kid's heart!

2. *Plan fun-filled activities ahead of time.* Kids quickly figure out if you're just making up silly stuff as you go. And when they think you're ad-libbing, your group will create their own version of silliness—and you may lose control. A group out of control results in chaos, and chaos is fun for no one.

3. *Kids enjoy leaders who personally engage in group activities.* If the lesson includes a game, make sure you play. After giving instructions about creating a picture collage, grab the glue and scissors so you can cut and paste. If your program includes worship music, then sing and do the accompanying motions. Your group won't care if you hit every note or how well you move, as I've learned from years of experience. Kids enjoy a leader who has fun with them much more than a leader who watches from the sidelines.

Season	Key word	Skills/actions
Summer	Fun	Exhibit a good attitude. Plan fun-filled activities ahead of time. Personally engage in group activities.

Fall: Life Change

Next comes a season known for change, so *life change* will serve as our key words to remember. During fall, plants reach their full height, leaves turn their brightest colors, and fields become ready for harvest. But all of this change took time, and the same is true in ministry.

Although life change sometimes happens quickly, it most often involves a slower, more subtle process—one that requires a leader's patience. In practical terms, patience emerges as the key ingredient in three important skills.

1. *Watch children closely for indications that spiritual growth is taking place.* Observing a child earnestly pray obviously belongs in this category. Also pay attention to other, more subtle cues—such as when a child enthusiastically partic-

ipates in worship, offers to help others, or begins involvement in volunteer opportunities. If you see these or other signs, affirm the child. To catch a momentary glimpse of life change requires a leader's patience in the form of willingness to pay attention during the times when nothing new appears.

2. *Listen closely to what children say.* This is closely related to the skill of watching. Remember those open-ended questions? Make sure you pay close attention to how kids respond to what you ask. This requires a leader to patiently stay in the present moment and resist the urge to think ahead to the next question or group exercise. Great leaders catch words that indicate life change because they listen. Then they use that information to help steer the meeting.

3. *Respond carefully to questions that kids ask.* Follow the wisdom of James 1:19: "Be quick to listen, slow to speak." Blurting out a quick response to a child's question might make a leader believe he has demonstrated a command of Scripture, but what happens if there's more to the question that can't be asked because the leader has started to talk? Mark Rook, a veteran leader in our second- and third-grade room, told me that the key to success as a leader is to resist the urge to speak, and to wait for just the right time to answer a question.

Great leaders like Mark know that a simple "Hmm" after a question provides plenty of runway for the second half of a question to land. Often a child's real interest emerges when she has an opportunity to elaborate on why the question came to mind. And *that* qualifies as "just the right time."

In fact, silence serves as a useful tool at many points during a group meeting. Kids need time to make up their minds and draw conclusions after a challenging question, but they can't do either if the leader continues to talk. And sometimes a quiet moment is the only response that honors a deeply personal statement offered by a group member.

It may take some practice to make sure you don't unintentionally inhibit profound moments from occurring through constant talk. Although it's difficult to resist the urge to move a meeting forward when the air goes still, great leaders know the power of being quiet so kids will talk. Or so that God can be heard.

Season	Key word	Skills/actions
Fall	Life change	Watch closely. Listen closely. Respond carefully; be silent when needed.

Winter: Warmth

For the final season the key word is *warmth*—which is what many people seek during winter. A warm group experience encourages the development of relationships, an important ministry ingredient. From his experience as children's pastor of Saddleback Church in southern California, Craig Jutila observes, "Kids come here for the program, but they stay because of relationships."[3]

Although Craig's West Coast climate stays warm throughout the year, two types of warmth deserve attention by group leaders—whether you live in Lake Forest, California, or Lake Placid, New York.

1. *Group warmth occurs when leaders create an emotionally safe and spiritually safe environment.* Specifically, this means the leader will constantly police against personal ridicule, negative comments, or hurtful humor—from other children or adults. Kids receive enough of this treatment elsewhere in life.

   Additionally, ensure that the group welcomes all questions, doubts, and confusion. Bob Merrill, a leader I served beside for two years, created a very open environment when he would ask the group, "C'mon guys, who really believes this?" in reference to the day's lesson. This simple question signaled that doubts or disbeliefs were okay. He then had an open door to address what the boys in the group really thought. Bob realized that we can offer a unique place for kids to safely process spiritual issues. Remember, life can feel awfully unsafe for kids.

2. *Leaders create personal warmth when they connect individually with each child.* To start, make sure everyone has an opportunity to participate in activities and discussions. This requires you to limit the participation of more outspoken children at times to make way for quieter group members. Offer the opportunity to join in the discussion as a true option, though, so you don't force any child out of his or her comfort zone.

Next, make a deliberate effort to communicate with each kid at least once (and ideally, more) in addition to the interaction they receive during group time. Options include making a phone call or mailing a card on a birthday, sending an encouraging note when the child faces a challenging week, or joining parents to attend a sports event or dance recital. Our children's ministry has stacks of cards for many occasions available to group leaders—including stamped envelopes! The sixty seconds required to jot a few words and write an address might warm a child's heart for weeks.

> The sixty seconds required to jot a few words and write an address might warm a child's heart for weeks.

For more immediate impact, look kids in the eye when you talk with them. You might need to go down on one knee to do it, depending on age—the child's and that of your knees. But this simple act will say to a child, "I believe you are important enough to give you my full attention." What kid doesn't love an adult's full attention?

Mark, the leader we heard about a moment ago, shared another approach to personal warmth while he and I chatted one Sunday morning. We'd only been talking for a few minutes, when he looked away from me and said to one of his group members, "Hi, Nathan. I'm glad you're back today." After another moment he said, "Hey Zachary, how are you this morning?" Later he said hello to Tony and gave him a high five. Mark showed me that a leader can create personal warmth by greeting kids by name and with a smile — making all of them feel you've waited all week to see them.

3. *A warm tone of voice will build personal trust.* Finally, remember that *how* you talk with kids will either reinforce or repeal the message of the words you say. "We believe tone of voice more than [we believe] the words that are spoken," says Karyn Henley in *Child-Sensitive Teaching.*[4] Great leaders treat their voices and nonverbal gestures as teaching tools.

Season	Key word	Skills/actions
Winter	Warmth	Create group warmth. Create personal warmth. Use vocal warmth.

ALL SEASONS, ONE CHILD

Several years ago I responded to a nudge by God to increase my volunteer involvement at our church, a path that took me into a dual role in Promiseland. I helped lead a small group as I partnered with a boy named Jimmy, who had some complex medical challenges that permanently confined him to a wheelchair. In this partnership, I helped him fully participate in our children's ministry program by physically compensating for his legs and right arm—which his condition had stricken. Because a significant portion of Promiseland takes place in small groups, I helped lead the group that Jimmy and I participated in every year.

Over the four-year period that Jimmy and I spent together, I learned firsthand about the impact the skill sets we've covered can make on an individual life. As we look back at specific examples of the four seasons in action, notice that while those skills can appear very different from situation to situation, they fundamentally remain the same.

Spring. One of the first things I discovered about Jimmy was his fear of sudden, loud noises. So we worked out a solution in which we locked eyes while I spoke words to help him remain calm. Those words needed to be the *right* ones for him, and they were specifically chosen to help him grow. "I'm right here, Jimmy," I said. "And God is right here with us too."

After our first few Sundays together, Jimmy's family had a schedule conflict, so they didn't attend church. Bob, the official small group leader, took the opportunity to talk with the group about Jimmy. I explained how it felt for him to be different—even in small ways such as everyone could sit on the floor except him. The boys received words of affirmation for specific ways they welcomed Jimmy into their group. They also heard instructions from me to keep their hands off his wheelchair!

Summer. Worship music plays a key part in Promiseland most weekends, and most songs include motions that kids find fun because they involve legs, arms, hands, and sometimes your whole body. That presents a challenge to people in wheelchairs. But not for Jimmy.

"I want to dance," he told me as a high-energy song started.

"You want to what?" I replied, somewhat flustered.

He locked his chair's wheels and repeated, "I want to dance—pick me up."

So from behind I reached under his arms and lifted him. And then we began to move to the motions with everyone else. Four hops to the right, four hops to the left. Throughout the song, and those that followed, I held Jimmy out in front of me and served as his legs. Because I have the rhythm of a flat tire, we fought hard to keep up with the music. But we somehow managed. And due to a young boy's desire to participate, my heart inflated with appreciation for worship. The next morning the pain in my back nearly kept me in bed. From that day on through the next four years, I prepared for the fun of worship through a consistent regimen of back exercises.

Another way we had fun was that I always called him "chief." I can still picture his eyes beaming when he heard "Hey, chief." I remember the feeling that my eyes, too, lit up whenever I called him that special name.

Fall. My experience with Jimmy stretched me in the area of careful responses to questions, mainly because some were tough to answer. For instance, I paused a long time after he asked, "If God hears my prayers, why can't I walk?" The only answer that seemed honest and biblical was "I don't know." At that moment, though, I saw a young boy who now wrestled with the thoughts of someone truly seeking to learn about God on a personal level.

I also saw clear change in the hearts of the group's other boys. One memorable moment came the weekend after we talked with the group about Jimmy. On their own initiative, they found chairs and brought them into our group room so that everyone was sitting—meaning Jimmy wouldn't feel different.

Winter. When Jimmy had surgery that offered hope for his ability to gain strength in his legs, Bob and I went to the hospital. When he woke from the anesthetic, Jimmy saw me and said he was scared. I would be too if I opened my eyes and saw both legs in casts from hip to toes. So we locked eyes, just like in Promiseland, and I spoke words to calm him down. I reminded him that I was there and—most importantly—God was with him too. Our relationship and personal interaction during ministry paid off in that hospital room.

Throughout the years we partnered, I sent him birthday cards and even went to a couple birthday celebrations. And I'll always remember a special gift he gave me.

After Jimmy's surgery he entered physical therapy, driven by the chance he might someday walk a few steps. About six months later, in early December, he met me when I arrived in Promiseland and announced that he had a present for me. His mom was with him, and she locked the wheels of his chair. Until that moment, he had not taken any steps outside of his therapist's office. But there, in front of a small crowd gathered around us, he took three small steps right into my arms!

A SPECIAL GIFT FOR LEADERS

Your motivation to lead a great group is that you will have the privilege to watch children, one by one, take steps in their walks with Jesus. Sometimes those strides will be little, unsure shuffles. Sometimes they'll be giant leaps of faith. Whatever the size, you get to be there, cheering them on. Ministry is a gift to all involved.

> Your motivation to lead a great group is that you will have the privilege to watch children, one by one, take steps in their walks with Jesus.

In his book *Here and Now*, author Henri Nouwen says, "Ministry is, first of all, receiving God's blessing from those to whom we minister. What is this blessing? It is a glimpse of the face of God.... We can see God in the face of Jesus, and we can see the face of Jesus in all those who need our care."[5] In the opinion of those in children's ministry, this blessing is even greater when it involves a precious child.

Expanding upon Henri's thought, one of my church's children's ministry volunteers wrote a poem that describes a special gift we receive through working with kids.

> **Because...**
>
> *When I laugh with a child at something silly,*
> *when I comfort a child and the crying stops,*
> *when we marvel together at something amazing,*
> *or when a child feels loved by me...*
>
> *If I look in that child's eyes,*
> *if the child looks back at me,*
> *if I look at just the right angle,*
> *and if I really let myself...*

I can see the eyes of Christ,
only for a split second,
but there they are.
It's hard for me to fully understand how,
and even tougher to explain why,
but there they are.

And every time this happens,
this brief glimpse of Jesus in a child's eyes,
I know I'm forever changed.

Because Jesus is looking back at me.

This weekend, look deeply into the eyes of the kids you lead or work with. You will see why the four seasons of leadership skills matter. You will know that your preparation and prayers are worth every moment. And I predict you will feel a new sense of confidence and conviction to give it your best when you remember the core belief underlying this chapter: *You can be a great group leader if you believe that Jesus is present in your group.*

Personal Exercise

In the chart below, write key words that describe deliberate actions you want to take to develop as a group leader:

Season	Key word	Suggested skills/actions	Actions I will take
Spring	Growth	Make statements that plant seeds of spiritual truth. Ask open-ended questions. Offer words of affirmation.	
Summer	Fun	Exhibit a good attitude. Plan fun-filled activities ahead of time. Personally engage in group activities.	
Fall	Life change	Watch closely. Listen closely. Respond carefully; be silent when needed.	
Winter	Warmth	Create group warmth. Create personal warmth. Use vocal warmth.	

CHAPTER 9

Expect Questions

M y family gathered around the kitchen table to plan a trip to San Diego. The thought of missing two days of school thrilled Scott, age seven. Five-year-old Erin looked forward to a long ride on a big jet. My wife, Becky, age not important, enthusiastically embraced the idea of a three-night hotel stay. Then I offered an idea that elevated everyone's excitement up a notch: "While we're there, let's go to Sea World!"

Earlier in the day, I had explored the Web to research our vacation destination. Now, armed with the details and descriptions one expects from a travel agent, I explained how Sea World mixes the fun of an amusement park with the wonder and intrigue of a zoo. All eyes around the table grew as I painted a picture of thrilling rides, trained dolphins, and Shamu the killer whale. Although our family enjoys attractions that require seat belts and restraining bars, the animals captured the most interest. Sea lions and giant turtles and polar bears—oh my!

As bedtime approached, we brought the family meeting to a close. I figured we were ready to conclude after thirty minutes of building high fascination for our next vacation. However, Erin posed one last question that caught everyone by surprise: "Are any of the animals real?"

In his book *Always Kiss Me Good Night—Instructions on Raising the Perfect Parent*, J. S. Salt compiled parenting advice from 147 kids. One child gave clear and simple counsel: "Help me with stuff I don't understand."[1] Obviously my daughter Erin needed similar help to comprehend a key part of our vacation.

That process began when she asked about the animals. As a children's ministry worker, Sunday school teacher, Christian educator, parent, or other faith influencer, prepare yourself for questions that children ask so you can help them with stuff they don't understand.

So why don't kids' questions always cause excitement in adults? Two of the most common reasons have to do with a reluctance to get off-task in the face of unexpected questions, and the fear of appearing biblically illiterate when handling difficult questions. A closer look at both issues will help calibrate our understanding of the critical role questions play in all ministry to children, and equip us to overcome our reluctance and fear.

> As a children's ministry worker, Sunday school teacher, Christian educator, parent, or other faith influencer, prepare yourself for questions that children ask so you can help them with stuff they don't understand.

FACING UNEXPECTED QUESTIONS

While leading a third-grade boys' small group discussion one Sunday morning, I saw that we had only a minute of time left and said, "Guys, let's pray before your parents come from big church." The lesson plan specifically called for a prayer, and our group had finished every other activity for the day.

Before I started the prayer, one boy asked, "Mr. Dave, how can God hear all the groups pray if everyone prays at the same time?"

Did I stop to address his question and explain that God has the ability to hear all prayers? No. Did I take a moment and say that God has so much love for every person that he wants to listen to each of us? No. Did the thought even enter my mind that this might be an opportune moment to discuss a spiritual topic of genuine interest to this boy and others in the group? No. I maintained clear focus on the task in front of me and said, "Let's not talk about that now because we need to pray." After "Amen," the parents arrived to pick up their kids—and that question never came back to mind until years later as I wrote this chapter.

That incident serves to illustrate what happens when a question comes at a seemingly inconvenient time. A leader has the day's lesson planned, and a question might distract the group from the agenda. I know firsthand that frustration too frequently becomes the common, unfortunate reaction to

unexpected questions. Being strongly task-oriented can leave little or no room for spontaneity—and questions, of course, tend to be spontaneous interruptions.

The solution is a conscious effort to welcome questions with enthusiasm, knowing that kids very often inquire because they have a desire to know or better understand. At its core, children's ministry seeks to help kids know and better understand God. To that end, questions indicate progress and should always be taken seriously. A German proverb says, "To question a wise man is the beginning of wisdom."[2] Let's resist the urge to feel frustrated when asked "Why?" for the umpteenth time or when sincere questions slow down—maybe even detour—a lesson or devotional. In fact, let's go so far as to be wary if a child *never* asks questions about God, Jesus, the Holy Spirit, heaven, or other spiritual topics—because that could mean a lack of interest or comprehension.

> Questions often signal a faith turning point because the questioner likely has an open, inquisitive mind about spiritual matters.

Willingness to spend a few extra moments to clarify concepts or provide further information might create an impact that extends for years—or an entire lifetime. In chapter 3 we read Megan's testimony about becoming a Christian as a fourth grader. Her second sentence below deserves special attention:

> I started going to Promiseland when I was in second grade. *I had a really nice leader who answered a lot of my questions.* Finally, in fourth grade, I admitted that I sin and believed that Jesus died for my sins. Then I asked Jesus to be my forever friend—and he still is.

Questions often signal a faith turning point because the questioner likely has an open, inquisitive mind about spiritual matters. The book of Acts contains numerous examples of queries posed just ahead of decisions to follow Jesus:

- Acts 2:37—An unidentified person asks, "Brothers, what shall we do?" following Peter's impromptu sermon on Pentecost. Three thousand people became Christians that day.

- Acts 8:34—The Ethiopian eunuch asks Philip, "Tell me, please, who is the prophet talking about, himself or someone else?" A conversation about Jesus follows, as does a conversion and the eunuch's baptism.

- Acts 9:5—On the Damascus road, Saul asks, "Who are you, Lord?" Jesus himself answers Saul, who becomes a Christ-follower and devotes his life to sharing Jesus with others.

- Acts 16:30—A Roman jailer asks Paul and Silas, "Sirs, what must I do to be saved?" The jailer and his family accept Christ, experience baptism that very night, and become part of Europe's first church in their hometown of Philippi.

HANDLING DIFFICULT QUESTIONS

It is obvious during our ministry's efforts to recruit volunteers that questions serve as a common reason people take a pass on joining our team. Many people fear they will be put on the spot with children's inquiries and not know how to adequately or eloquently respond. At the heart of this concern sits the anxiety of appearing biblically illiterate. Fortunately there are ways to eliminate such fear.

Everyone who spends time around children knows that kids ask about a variety of topics—sometimes in the same breath. Even narrowing the parameters to Christianity doesn't trim the potential questions down to a manageable number. So for the purposes of this discussion, let's primarily focus on inquiries related to salvation, the most important spiritual issues kids are likely to ask about. A long list of questions and answers to memorize, though, would provide only limited preparation. A few basic skills will prove more effective and longer lasting.

An ancient Chinese proverb says, "Give a man a fish and he'll eat for a day. Teach him to fish and you'll feed him for life."[3] If we equate answering questions to catching fish, learning the three following approaches will equip us to face a multitude of questions. While we examine each of these three, we'll also reel in some of the most frequently asked questions that adults in children's ministry will likely hear. Hopefully, you'll find the suggested answers to be keepers.

Approach 1 — Direct Response

At first glance, this approach seems simple to imagine — just answer the question. However, during a focus group with several veteran leaders in our ministry's small group structure, three guidelines to the direct response approach emerged. All fit under an umbrella of logic labeled, "Answer questions carefully."

First, refer to the Bible either verbally or physically whenever possible. As an example, assume a child asks, "If God loves everyone, won't all people go to heaven?" In this case, you can verbally reference Scripture: "You are right that God loves everyone. The Bible says in the book of John that he loves us so much that he sent his only Son Jesus as the way for people to go to heaven. This means that everyone who believes in Jesus will go there. God gives everyone the choice to believe in him, and the chance to go to heaven." Another way to respond would be to say, "Let's look in the Bible together for the answer." Then turn to John 3:16 and read aloud (the child or you). This might turn into a discussion about whether or not the child believes in Jesus. Make sure, though, that when you suggest looking in the Bible together that you have a good idea where to look or the child may perceive Scripture as a difficult place to find answers.

The second guideline is to consider whether the question asked is the *real* issue. In the book *101 Questions Chil-*

dren Ask about God, the authors encourage, "Look for the question behind the question. For example, when a little boy asks, 'Does the devil have claws?' he probably wants to know, 'Can the devil hurt me?' "[4] The question we examined earlier about God's love and everyone going to heaven could indicate a child's confusion about the salvation plan. The answer should include a very simple and clear description of how people go to heaven. And it should be made personal by using "you" and "I" instead of "people" and "everyone." Understanding the underlying issue will help us provide a specific response and resist the ever-present temptation to over-answer the question.

The third guideline encourages us to be sensitive to the emotions behind questions, and to acknowledge those emotions in our responses. For example, the question "Do all people go to heaven?" obviously needs delicate handling when you know that someone close to the child has recently passed away. I've seen relief wash over the face of a kid when he hears, "It can be scary to not know for sure about someone when they pass away. But even though we can't see what they truly believed in their hearts—God can."

A child might also feel guilty about something she did, which prompts the common query: "Do I have to pray for Jesus to forgive me every time I do something wrong? If I don't, will I still go to heaven?" For this inquiry, offer the formula for relief (based on Romans 10:9) in your answer: "I wonder that too when I feel bad about something I've done. But the Bible says that once you've asked Jesus to be your forever friend, you're sure to go to heaven. The Bible also says, though, that we need to continually tell God about the wrong stuff we do. And because he sees everything we do, he already knows about it anyway. So he's just waiting for us to say 'I'm sorry' so he can remind us that he forgives us. You can pray to God anytime to ask him to forgive you for anything you've done. He likes it when we say that kind of prayer."

Approach 2 — No-Answer Response

There will be times when the honest answer is no answer, either because you don't know or the Bible is silent on the issue. The words "I don't know" or "the Bible doesn't say" communicate honesty, not incompetence. Although tempting, resist the urge to craft a quick direct response just to appear smart or to say words that a child wants to hear.

I don't know.

Bible story highlights seem easy to remember, as do the core lessons those stories teach. The details that surround those stories, though, can pose a challenge. Questions about specific facts can pop into a child's mind and stay there building up pressure until he has the opportunity to ask. I experienced this one Sunday morning when I served as a small group leader.

The day's lesson focused on the story of Noah, which I know well. At least that's the confident thought I had for the first few minutes of group discussion. Then a young girl quickly humbled me by asking, "Did Noah know that the rain was coming before he made the boat?" The correct answer is yes, according to Genesis 6:13–17. Unfortunately, though, my memory failed at the very moment I needed to recall that detail. When I asked a group of leaders what they would do in a scenario like this, they suggested that I say, "That's a great question, and I'm not really sure. I'll look for an answer in the Bible and let you know what I find." This response communicates to the child that her question has value, and also shows how to use the Bible as a resource. What must follow, of course, is quality investigation so that the child receives a timely answer.

> The words "I don't know" or "the Bible doesn't say" communicate honesty, not incompetence.

The Bible is silent.

Occasionally, questions arise that the Bible does not clearly or completely address. "We don't always know about everything God does and does not do, but we can still pray about it," is a response that models authenticity and yet still points the child toward approaching God with his concern. Questions in this category tend to involve specific situations such as: "I prayed for my grandma to get better, and she still isn't. Why?" Bob Gustafson, a Promiseland veteran teacher/leader, suggests this answer: "You must love your grandma very much to pray for her. We don't know why God chooses to answer some of our prayers the way we hope, and why sometimes he doesn't. Just because your prayer hasn't been answered the way you hoped doesn't mean God didn't hear you or that you should stop praying for your grandma."

Pointing to nearby truth offers another response strategy when the Bible is silent on an issue: "That's a question I wonder about too, and I don't know. But we can know this ..." This approach works well when you know that the Bible clearly addresses a topic very closely related to the original question.

For example, surveys in our ministry show that the spiritual question kids most frequently ask is whether or not their pets will go to heaven. People have opinions on this issue, but the Bible provides no definitive answer. Additionally, the most predictable time a child will ask is following the loss of a loved animal. An appropriate response requires comfort and substance because fragile feelings exist.

"It's real sad when you lose a pet, sort of like losing a real good friend, isn't it? I've felt that way before too. You can pray and ask God to help you not feel so sad. The Bible never clearly says what happens to pets when they die. But God created all animals, so he knows. What we do know is that the Bible says that when we get to heaven we'll experience great joy."

Beth Bauer, Promiseland's director of small group life, says, "This type of response evens the playing field between the adult and child by validating and valuing the question as well as the child himself." Showing kids this respect yields relational and developmental benefits for both the short and long term.

"Questioning is a key component of a spiritual life," says Betsy Taylor in *What Kids Want That Money Can't Buy*. "Our role as loving parents is to honor the questions, nurture the life-long search for — and experience of — truth and wisdom, and create the conditions for a positive spiritual life."[5] Although she directs her counsel to moms and dads, Betsy's message applies to all of us who work with kids. Through honoring a child's questions, we show the child how much we value him or her — even when the answer is "I don't know."

Approach 3 — Ask a Question

When I think back to my school-age years, I can remember specific teachers quite skilled at pulling knowledge out of me. A common tactic used by these adept educators was to reply to questions with questions. This method typically prompted me to discover the answer through dialogue that followed — or provided the teacher with more information that generated a crisp, high-impact answer. The greatest teacher, Jesus, frequently practiced this method — and three variations of his approach appear highly transferable into children's ministry.

Explain, please.

One of them, named Cleopas, asked him, "Are you only a visitor to Jerusalem and do not know the things that have happened there in these days?"

"What things?" he asked.

"About Jesus of Nazareth," they replied. "He was a prophet, powerful in word and deed before God and all the people."

Luke 24:18–19

In this passage, Jesus asks a question ("What things?") that requires Cleopas and his friends to elaborate on what they are talking about. In ministry when a child asks a very broad question, we can ask for clarification of the question, for clues about the expected answer, or for the inquisitor to provide additional insight on the motivation behind the question.

For example, a broad question kids commonly ask is, "How do you know there really is a God?" Potential responses that follow the *Explain, please* method include: "That's an interesting question—how do *you* think we know?" or "That's a big question—what makes you ask?" Both options initiate dialogue that will likely prove more valuable than quickly answering the question. And they may well uncover information to help you develop an appropriate response.

You know.

Some Pharisees came and tested him by asking, "Is it lawful for a man to divorce his wife?"

"What did Moses command you?" he replied.

Mark 10:2–3

On one occasion an expert in the law stood up to test Jesus. "Teacher," he asked, "what must I do to inherit eternal life?"

"What is written in the Law?" he replied. "How do you read it?"

Luke 10:25–26

These two examples show how Jesus skillfully helped people recall information they already know—information that begins to answer the original question. In both passages the questioner expects a very brief response, but Jesus knows the answer is far from simple. Whenever a child can discover the answer on her own—or at least contribute information along the way toward a thorough response—comprehension and retention will remain high.

Let's look again at the question "How do you know there really is a God?" Responding with, "What signs do you think people *could* see that God exists?" will prompt a child to share evidence of God's existence familiar to her—a great discussion starting point. The *You know* method also helps alleviate tension from confrontational questions.

Different angle.

> "Tell us then, what is your opinion? Is it right to pay taxes to Caesar or not?"
>
> But Jesus, knowing their evil intent, said, "You hypocrites, why are you trying to trap me? Show me the coin used for paying the tax." They brought him a denarius, and he asked them, "Whose portrait is this? And whose inscription?"
>
> "Caesar's," they replied.
>
> Then he said to them, "Give to Caesar what is Caesar's, and to God what is God's."
>
> Matthew 22:17–21

Even though children asking questions have no evil intent, we can see from Jesus' example the value of asking about a different, yet directly related issue that points to the answer. This method will help engage serious thought as long as the connection becomes clear between the response question you pose and the original question asked.

> Whenever you ask a question in response to a question, avoid the conversational loop "I asked you," "But I asked you first."

Once again let's use the question "How do you know there really is a God?" Potential responses could point toward evidence of God's presence in everyday things the child sees. Examples of questions to ask include the following: "If you look all around us, how do you think a world filled with so many living things began?" "What do you think makes things come alive and grow?" Or "Who do you think made people so different from all the animals?" When using *Different angle* you might hear "I don't know," which opens the door for you and the child to discover the answer together ("Let's think about that for a moment") and then relate back to the original question.

Whenever you ask a question in response to a question, avoid the conversational loop "I asked you," "But I asked you first," which may occur when you appear to be avoiding the question. If this pattern starts, simply provide a direct answer and prompt further dialogue by asking, "Does that seem right to you?" or "So what does that answer make you think about?"

Parents and Questions

Ministry leaders I spoke with agree that with some questions kids ask, you may want to share the question with the child's parents with the child present. When prefaced by a positive, nearly congratulatory tone, such as, "Your daughter asked a great question today," a youngster will feel valued and practically brilliant. The possibility is now open for a continued spiritual conversation at home. Of course steer clear of this idea when the question ties back to a relational issue with the parent, or if sharing the question will break a confidence.

On the topic of parents, leaders in Promiseland hear common questions from them too. One of the most frequent ones is, "How do I know if my child really started a relationship with Jesus?" Although the ultimate answer to this question rests between the child and God, that response won't minister well to the parent. Instead, reply with either or both of the following:

"Can she describe, using her own words, what she did and what it means to her?"

"Can you see discernible life change in him?"

If the honest answer is no, then partner with the parent to determine the best course to follow. Perhaps another salvation explanation should take place or the parent could share his or her testimony with the child. Possibly more time needs to pass for a younger child to mature. Or maybe explore another opportunity to say the A-B-C prayer. Whatever the next step, agree to pray for the child and to encourage questions.

Between home and church, kids will have all the chances they need to ask their questions, right? Not always. For a variety of reasons—including limited time or shyness—kids wonder about more than they ask. To keep a pulse on kids' thoughts, our ministry periodically surveys them. We've found strong willingness from kids to submit more questions in writing than they ask aloud. Teachers and leaders then review the list to assure that lesson content addresses frequently appearing issues. This practice also helps small group leaders prepare for questions they might hear. You will find the results of one such survey in appendix 6.

A commitment to answering questions stems from the belief that a child can be one question and answer away from understanding a key truth that will open into a relationship with Jesus. While our family planned a visit to Sea World, my daughter asked a question because she wanted to know if the animals we described were real. When she found out they were, she became excited enough to tell everyone she saw about our vacation plans. As children sit through programs every week they will wonder, too, if what we say about Christianity is real. When we effectively answer their questions, and they discover God's plan is true, that news will be so exciting they'll want to share it with everyone they know.

Quick Reference Guide to Approaching Kids' Questions

1. Direct Response

   a. Refer to the Bible either verbally or physically whenever possible

   b. Consider whether the question asked is the real issue

   c. Be sensitive to the emotion behind the question

2. No-Answer Response

   a. I don't know

   b. The Bible is silent

3. Ask a Question

   a. Explain, please

   b. You know

   c. Different angle

Personal Exercise

Complete the following chart with your ideas for appropriate answers or other words to use that differ from those used in this chapter — while maintaining kid-appropriateness. For additional practice, respond to the broader list of questions found in appendix 6.

Frequently heard question	Answer from chapter	My answer
"If God loves everyone, won't all people go to heaven?"	"You are right that God loves everyone. The Bible says in the book of John that he loves us so much that he sent his only Son Jesus as the way for people to go to heaven. This means that everyone who believes in him will go there. God gives everyone the choice to believe in Jesus, and the chance to go to heaven." (Bible reference — John 3:16)	
"Do all people go to heaven?"	"It can be scary to not know for sure about someone when they pass away. But even though we can't see what they truly believed in their hearts — God can." (Bible reference — Romans 10:13)	

Frequently heard question	Answer from chapter	My answer
"Do I have to pray for Jesus to forgive me every time I do something wrong, and if I don't will I still go to heaven?"	"I wonder that too when I feel bad about something I've done. But the Bible says that once you've asked Jesus to be your forever friend, you're sure to go to heaven. The Bible also says, though, that we need to continually tell God about the wrong stuff we do. And because he sees everything we do, he already knows about it. So he's waiting for us to say 'I'm sorry' so that he can remind us that he forgives us. You can pray to God anytime to ask him to forgive you for anything you've done. He likes it when we say that kind of prayer." (Bible reference — Romans 10:9)	
"Will my pet go to heaven?"	"It's real sad when you lose a pet, sort of like losing a real good friend, isn't it? I've felt that way before too. You can pray and ask God to help you not feel so sad. The Bible never clearly says what happens to pets when they die. But God created all animals, so *he* knows. And we do know that the Bible says that when we get to heaven we'll experience great joy." (Bible reference — Genesis 1:25)	

Frequently heard question	Answer from chapter	My answer
"I prayed for my grandma to get better, and she still isn't. Why?"	"You must love your grandma very much to pray for her. We don't know why God chooses to answer some of our prayers the way we hope, and why sometimes he doesn't. Just because your prayer wasn't answered the way you thought doesn't mean God didn't hear you or that you should stop praying for your grandma."	
Bible details you can't recall on the spot: "Did Noah know that the rain was coming before he made the boat?"	"That's a great question, and I'm not really sure. I'll look for an answer in the Bible and let you know what I find."	
"How do you know there really is a God?"	"That's an interesting question; what do *you* think the answer is?" "What signs do you think people *could* see that God exists?" "If you look all around us, how do you think a world filled with so many living things began?"	

CHAPTER 10

The Power of Everyone

The toughest part of an amusement park visit is not the admission price. It's not the hours of waiting in lines, nor even the queasy feeling from a thrill ride. The most daunting challenge comes when you tell your family that it's time to leave. Kids (and dads) never want to go home because the park offers so much excitement. On a recent trip I decided that our day of fun must avoid the ugliness sure to come the moment I'd announce, "It's time to go." So I developed a plan.

For years my kids have gawked at people who walked past us carrying unusually large stuffed animals won in games scattered throughout the park. Each time they'd notice a three-foot bear, four-foot pink panther, or five-foot snake they'd offer guesses about which game the person won. At the same time, my wife and I quietly speculated about how many times the person had to try, multiplying that number by the typical cost of five dollars per chance. Then we'd announce better uses for that amount of money—purchasing a car, paying for college, and other possibilities that made a point about good stewardship. Those lectures ensured my plan would come as a surprise.

One hour into this particular visit, we spotted the first big game winner. Rather than launching into my typical, cynical remarks, I made an offer that shocked everyone. "Let's win a giant animal today," I said.

"Stop joking, Dad. You're not funny," my daughter, Erin, replied.

"I'm serious. Erin, you can pick the game and I'll win the animal. But we have to play the game on our way to the car so we won't have to carry the prize with us all day."

I've never seen my kids so willing to head home. All day they scouted for the game that offered the largest animal. When the moment came, Erin announced her choice—a basketball game called Bank-A-Shot. Fortunately for me, I've played basketball all my life. And I also know the secret to this particular game.

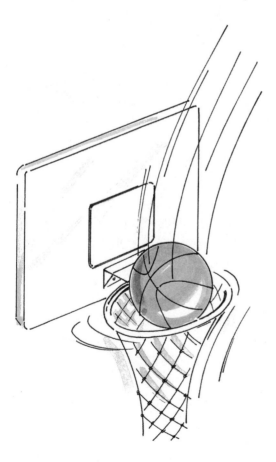

While my wife reluctantly handed the attendant five dollars, my daughter confirmed that to win the grand prize —a giant monkey—required me to make only one basket. I took a ball and backed away from the game a few feet so I could dribble and focus on the smaller-than-regulation basket. I also ignored the name of the game, knowing that the shot is nearly impossible to make by banking it in. The secret is to shoot the ball high so that it drops straight through the rim.

"Only one try," I announced to show confidence and also to protect myself from the potential financial disaster of multiple attempts. A crowd gathered. My heart raced. Pride was at stake. So was a huge stuffed monkey. I took a deep breath and shot the ball high. The crowd gasped. My wife's eyes were shut. Mine had tears in them. The world moved in slow motion. For an instant I even questioned the wisdom of my plan—until the shot went in!

After my daughter selected a bright blue monkey (which we named Mr. Hoops in honor of the occasion), our happy family walked through the exit. My plan worked, but only because I picked the right time to take my shot—and because the ball went in the basket.

Similarly, the right time—and the best shot—to introduce people to life with Christ presents itself during childhood. Researcher George Barna says, "Families, churches and parachurch ministries must recognize that [the] primary window of opportunity for effectively reaching people with the good news of Jesus' death and resurrection is during the pre-teen years. It is during those years that people develop their frames of reference for the remainder of their life—especially theologically and morally."[1]

> There will be times when you can make an eternal impact based on how you react— and someone will need you to do that well.

The secret to scoring with that best shot is simple: aim high. To do this, establish strong expectations for your ministry and invite participation from key people in your church. In this game, everyone is on the team and has a play to make.

STRONG MINISTRY EXPECTATIONS

As mentioned earlier, I consistently attended church through-out my childhood. I sat in the house of God every seven days for many years, surrounded by God's Word and good people who worked hard to ensure that church experience took place. For my entire childhood, I stood only one clear salvation explana-tion away from the possibility of giving my life to Jesus. Unfor-tunately, that explanation never came. No kid should come that close to Jesus and walk away without being changed—or without the children's ministry making a concerted effort to change that kid. But what does this look like? Ministries who set the following four clear expectations for themselves reflect a high level of effort to lead kids to Jesus:

1. We will present and discuss the plan.

A ministry can welcome kids every weekend, go through Bible lessons that teach plenty, and yet never share the need to make a decision about Jesus. A ministry committed to help-ing kids start relationships with Jesus, on the other hand, will regularly present clear, relevant, and creative salvation explana-tions—and then go the extra step of prompting personal dis-cussions. Ministries shoot too low when they focus on gospel presentations to large groups and then leave the opportunity for more intimate conversation unplanned or up to chance. Instead, consider allowing half the ministry hour for a corpo-rate experience, and spending the second half in smaller set-tings with carefully crafted discussion activities and questions that stimulate thought and discussion.

For example, our children's ministry teaches a salvation les-son called "Big Gift" for second and third graders. During a gathering of everyone in these two grades, kids experience a session that creatively explains God's gift of grace and the need to accept his offer. Immediately after this presentation, the lesson calls for time in small groups that builds off the large group teaching through discussion and an interactive activity. Leaders receive these detailed instructions:

SMALL GROUP LEADER'S NOTES

The intention of this time is to review and ask questions about what the kids learned today in Large Group. Whether a child is already a Christian or not, this will be an important time for each child to either learn for the first time or reaffirm what he or she already knows about God's forgiveness.

Testimony guide: Because the kids look to you as their leader, it is important for you to authentically share your testimony in a way they will understand. Prepare and review your story using these three guidelines:

1. (BC) Where were you spiritually before receiving Christ? What were you like? What caused you to consider God/Jesus?

2. (The cross) What realization did you come to that finally motivated you to make Jesus your forever friend? Specifically, remind the kids how you Admitted, Believed, and Chose to become a Christian.

3. (AD) How did your life begin to change after becoming a Christian?

LARGE GROUP REVIEW

ASK: "What was the Big Gift?"
ACTIVITY 1: LEADER'S STORY

SHARE how you asked Jesus to be your forever friend by using the guide above.
ACTIVITY 2: GOD'S STORY

TAKE out the God's Story Cards [small cards that show an image or key word that will act as visual prompts for reviewing concepts from the large group lesson]. Put one God's Story Card in the center of your group. Keep the rest of the cards facedown in your lap.

TELL the kids, "For some of you, this is the first time you are hearing about how to become a Christian. Some of you are already Christians, so this is a review. Either way, take this time to learn God's story so you can remember it and share it with friends and family. Let's review the story (presented in Large Group), and if you have any questions about the cards, feel free to ask as we go."

[further instructions follow that provide questions that correspond with each card]

©2001 Willow Creek Community Church.

2. We will shepherd kids.

Ed Young, senior pastor of Fellowship Church in Grapevine, Texas, understands how life change takes place in his church's children's ministry. "Small groups are critical for making an Adventure World Weekend a true success," he says in the book *Can We Do That?* "In Adventure World we have adult leaders who commit to leading small groups of kids during a special breakout session. In these small groups, the kids are helped to understand the life application of the lesson that is being taught that day."[3]

A key word in Ed's description deserves special attention: commitment. In Promiseland, we agree with that requirement. In fact, we ask small group leaders to show up all forty-two weekends during our ministry season, with ten weeks off during the summer. At the heart of this requirement rests a fundamental need: children will develop a trusting, open relationship only with an adult they routinely see.

When a small group leader proves to be reliable through consistent presence, kids become more likely to ask important questions, participate in discussion, share heart issues, and listen to what that adult says—including a personal testimony or scriptural truth. Effective shepherding takes place only when a familiar relationship exists. Certainly that concept has been around for a while. Jesus described the importance of familiarity with a shepherd in John 10:4–5: "When he has brought out all his own, he goes on ahead of them, and his sheep follow him because they know his voice. But they will never follow a

stranger; in fact, they will run away from him because they do not recognize a stranger's voice."

3. We will make salvation the mission.

Every children's ministry has an answer to the question "What does your ministry do?" In conversations with churches around the world, though, I've noticed that many respond with details about the curriculum they teach, the creeds and rituals their children memorize, and annual programs that have become time-honored traditions. Children's programs that aim high, however, respond with a better answer.

"We help kids become Christians" or some form of that statement indicates mission clarity. The children's ministry of Northwoods Community Church in Peoria, Illinois, provides an excellent example: "The mission of Discoveryland is to assist in the child's spiritual development so that, in God's time, the child will come to have a personal and growing relationship [with God] through Jesus Christ."[4]

> One clear indicator evaluates our effectiveness: decisions for Jesus either take place or they don't.

A ministry committed to helping kids start a relationship with Jesus doesn't keep it a secret and won't expect it to happen by chance. In his book *Turning Vision into Action*, George Barna says, "Mission is the grand purpose for which you or your ministry exists."[5] It is important that the congregation, church leaders, and volunteers all understand that the children's program—possibly held downstairs each weekend—operates with a grand purpose that reaches to heaven.

Look to the Great Commission in Matthew 28:19–20 and the mission of ministry becomes quite clear: Guide individuals into a relationship with Jesus ("Therefore go and make disciples of all nations, baptizing them in the name of the Father and of the Son and of the Holy Spirit, . . ."), and disciple people in their Christian walks (" . . . teaching them to obey everything that I have commanded you").

Jesus' Great Commission serves as the basis for Discoveryland's mission statement and for Promiseland's as well: "Supplement the family in reaching kids and helping them become fully devoted followers of Christ." If either ministry ever wavers from intentionality toward helping kids cross the line of faith, we will be off-mission. For us to do the job we have committed to do, we must constantly aim high—and one clear indicator evaluates our effectiveness: decisions for Jesus either take place or they don't.

When the entire ministry focuses on a common mission, then everyone can see how the role they play fits in the larger cause. Inspired small group leaders or teachers know the grand purpose of why they show up every weekend. Motivated early childhood workers understand that their counterparts in late childhood need them to lay a solid spiritual foundation in little kids—to be built on for years to come. And every time a child enters God's family, the whole ministry shares the joy of mission accomplished!

4. We will offer the right environment.

Picture your ministry from a child's eyes for a moment. Look at the halls, doors, floors, and corners. Now answer a key question from a youngster's perspective: When I compare this to all the other places I go, do I want to spend time here? This might seem like a silly exercise, but not if your ministry strives to aim high.

A child-targeted environment communicates to kids that they have found a place where they belong. To accomplish this, a ministry makes deliberate decisions about decor, music, teaching style, and activities that appeal to the children. If a boy or girl enters a room, looks around, and believes an environment exists for him or her, the result is a positive attitude that leads to openness and receptivity.

Want to check out this theory? Count the number of smiles on kids at an amusement park, McDonald's Funland, or on a playground. (Don't include your own as you tabulate.) Compare that number to those you see in a formal restaurant, a hardware store, or your church's main sanctuary. Which group is more inclined to hear what you have to say about Jesus? I'll take the smiles every time. You don't need to offer thrill rides or french fries to succeed in ministry, but you also can't expect to accomplish much in a dull setting.

Same goes for safety. Even though Christianity offers the greatest news the world has to offer, children will ignore that

message unless they feel at ease. A fully safe area has three dimensions: physical safety that assures kids they won't be harmed, emotional safety that protects children from ridicule and other devaluing actions, and spiritual safety that encourages faith questions and open discussions about real-life issues. Does your ministry offer all three? Schools don't, and neither do neighborhoods, nor a surprising number of homes. In fact, your children's ministry might be the only comprehensively safe place a kid experiences.

Of course that experience also requires fun. A children's ministry with a reputation for fun will radiate energy that magnetically attracts kids. Children naturally and almost effortlessly spread the news about an experience they enjoy. Jesus spoke of the joy he wants all his followers to feel: "I have told you this so that my joy may be in you and that your joy may be complete" (John 15:11). So let that feeling take place with kids. Hearts for Jesus will pound when laughter abounds.

Environments That Work

Northview Christian Life Church in Noblesville, Indiana, decided to build a dedicated children's facility and ended up with a dynamic environment for kids. From the moment boys and girls go down a giant slide to enter the classroom area, they know they belong. When families enter the hall that leads into the new building, they must pass through a computer check-in area which demonstrates a commitment to safety. Themed room decor, including a sports locker room and a fire department, helps kids have fun. And with life-changing ministry at their core, attendance continues to soar. However, creating the right environment need not require large budgets or construction.

Grace Community Church resides less than five miles away from Northview. The children's ministry team at Grace has done a great job converting very standard, rectangular rooms into bright, appealing environments that make kids' faces shine when they enter. They have areas designated for engaging activity stations, and implement solid security procedures on folding tables located in the hallway outside every room. When the room lights dim and yield to a few well-placed theater lights, creative stages capture attention and serve as effective platforms for strong Bible lessons and heartfelt worship. The result—lives changing and attendance growing.

> Regardless of the facility you occupy, your ministry can set and pursue clear expectations for itself—and more.

Northview and Grace have environments constructed differently, that vary considerably in cost and complexity, yet both deliver effective ministry in the right environment. And both aim high through dedicated time each week for small group discussions led by teams of adults committed to intentionally shepherding kids.

Regardless of the facility you occupy, your ministry can set and pursue clear expectations for itself—and more.

INVOLVE OTHER KEY PEOPLE

I've coached my son's basketball teams for five seasons. Each Tuesday evening we hold a one-hour practice and each Saturday we play a forty-minute game. Each of the boys I oversee fall into one of two groups. Youngsters who fall into the first group participate in those practices and games—and nothing else. The only time they pick up a basketball is in the gym with the team. Many times these young players—and their parents—wonder why their shots don't go in, passes go errant, and dribbles bounce off their feet.

The boys in the other group also attend the practices and compete in the games. In addition, they play basketball at home during the week. At the end of each season, the boys who have played more than just the weekly hour and forty minutes of our program reach skill levels far past the first group—especially if parents or older siblings have worked with them on the same fundamentals covered in practice. The game makes more sense and becomes more natural for those who play consistently.

Likewise, Christianity will make more sense and come more naturally for kids who frequently interact with faith issues. Your church has key people outside of your immediate ministry team who benefit from your ministry's success. These folks can add two important ingredients to help you cook up plenty of faith interaction for kids: consistency and involvement.

Pastoral Support

Children's consistent attendance serves as a foundation that makes building a relationship with God more likely. A commitment to high frequency will evolve into a churchwide value only when a church's pastor understands the benefit to kids and the ultimate responsibility of parents. In a weekend message, Menlo Park Presbyterian Church (Menlo Park, California) teaching pastor John Ortberg challenged moms and dads to take their responsibility for family-wide spiritual development seriously by telling the congregation: "Parents, do whatever you have to do ... because getting your kids into a consistent pattern of Promiseland attendance and involvement is the best help I think you can get with the most important parenting assignment you'll ever face."[6]

Attendance is an issue difficult to address by the children's ministry because its audience—kids—can't drive themselves to church. A church's pastor occupies the best platform to deliver this message, so periodically remind him or her of its value. If needed, photocopy the page with John Ortberg's quote, mark his words with a highlighter, and share it with your pastor.

Parental Involvement

After you've secured the pastor's active support, turn attention toward opportunities for your ministry to connect with parents. North Point Church in Atlanta offers a creative program called KidStuf that parents and kids attend together in the hour between Sunday services. After they experience a dynamic time of learning, families leave with materials designed to stimulate conversations during the days to come—even questions specifically for car rides. Learning launched on Sunday continues to fly Monday through Saturday, propelled by the reality that repetition is the key to learning.

Ministry opportunities that impact the home exist past offering shared experiences and physically distributing materials. Ed Young describes another successful strategy of Fellowship Church's Adventure World: "Small-group leaders are also challenged to maintain contact with the families of the children in their group beyond the confines of the church itself."[7] A leader can make a phone call to check on a youngster who's absent a few weeks in a row, send a birthday card, or attend a basketball game. We covered these ideas in chapter 8, but only in consideration of the impact on kids. All are easy. And all create connections with kids *and* their parents. Imagine how much more receptive children will be to a leader or teacher who has become a family friend—a person Mom or Dad knows and refers to by name. The expectation to set with parents is to be receptive to the leader's efforts. Similar to the attendance issue, your pastor can most effectively deliver the message about receptivity.

> Parents, the children's ministry, and church leadership share a commitment to stand shoulder-to-shoulder and unleash the power of everyone.

A ministry's efforts to partner with parents will be well received. In every parent-teacher conference I've attended, I ask the same question: "What can we do at home to help Erin (or Scott) succeed in your class?" If parents will adjust home life so that kids can better learn math, reading, and writing, won't parents take steps to help kids learn the most important lesson in life—the need for a relationship with Jesus? The answer is yes when parents, the children's ministry, and church leadership share a commitment to stand shoulder-to-shoulder and unleash the power of everyone.

Working together takes place when strong and clear expectations exist. Ministries and parents jointly own responsibility to aim this timely "shot"—to help kids know Jesus—as high as we can shoot it. But that's where our responsibility ends: God determines if the ball goes in the basket—whether or not a relationship with Jesus starts.

Today Mr. Hoops sits in a corner of my daughter's room and acts as a trophy for a one-time victory. Unfortunately, most people who play amusement park games leave empty-handed. Ministry, however, operates under different rules with a different prize system. When we give our best efforts—when we do all we can to lead children to Jesus—the Bible guarantees we win: "Everyone ... who acknowledges me before others, I also will acknowledge before my Father in heaven" (Matthew 10:32 NRSV).

Personal Exercises

1. Application question: Does your ministry clearly present the salvation plan and offer kids the opportunity to respond? Describe when and where. If yes, do lessons call for critical participation from small group leaders?

2. Describe the commitment your ministry expects from group leaders who shepherd kids. Is that level in the best interest of kids, or is it intentionally low to serve adults?

3. How does your ministry's mission compare with the Great Commission (Matthew 28:19–20)

4. Rate your ministry on a scale of one to five in the following areas (one low, five high):

Child targeted	1	2	3	4	5
Safe	1	2	3	4	5
Fun	1	2	3	4	5
Parental connection	1	2	3	4	5

Ask four parents to rate the ministry and provide you with specific observations for your attention. Discuss the results with your team and brainstorm ways to improve. Repeat this exercise annually.

5. To help parents develop the same skills covered in this book, suggest they read *Leading Your Child to Jesus*.

A Final Word

This book focused a lot of attention on words because they are potent tools. The Bible reinforces this truth repeatedly. God uses words to create the world ("God said, 'Let there be light,' and there was light," Genesis 1:3), trigger miracles ("just say the word, and my servant will be healed," Matthew 8:8), and provide truth that transcends time ("Heaven and earth will pass away, but my words will never pass away," Matthew 24:35).

Our journey together began with an awareness that what we say and how we say it will increase our effectiveness in leading kids to Jesus. The pages that followed those introductory thoughts provided examples, suggestions, and practical strategies that—I pray—will help you speak clearly and with impact. Ideally, you now possess abundant passion and steadfast belief that when you lock eyes with a child, the words you speak can make a real difference. Church on the Way pastor Jack Hayford says, "It is perhaps among the most humbling features of God's ways with humankind that He confers upon us a staggering degree of power (and responsibility) in the capacity of our words to cause things to happen."[1]

Let's remain realistic, though, with what we can accomplish through skillful language use. Even the most eloquent, age-appropriate, kid-sensitive discussion will fall short of success on its own. That's because every conversation intended to usher a child into a life with the Lord and an eternity spent in heaven requires the power that comes from a single Word. And in that Word alone rests the ability to change lives and the hope of the world:

> *In the beginning was the Word, and the Word was with God, and the Word was God.*
>
> John 1:1

Four Key Dynamics
of Communicating with Kids

Dynamic 1—**Children understand concrete terms and language better than they understand abstract terms and language.** Children are likely to be much more literal with language than adults, so avoid symbolism or "religious" words.

Dynamic 2—**Children are at different developmental levels.** Age is a factor in a child's ability to understand, no matter how simply worded a concept might be communicated. A child's age will partner with such factors as education, family and social surroundings, and life experiences to influence his or her intellect and spiritual knowledge.

Dynamic 3—**Children are most receptive to stories and terms they can relate to or picture.** No one, especially a child, enjoys a lecture. Kids will understand far more of what an adult attempts to explain when that adult uses a brief story. Children will also engage with what's said at a deeper level when a leader or teacher uses words that refer to something familiar to them—creating a connection between the story and the listener.

Dynamic 4—**Children may focus on, or be distracted by, a single detail in a story.** Carefully consider details you share in a story told to kids. Reexamine details to be sensitive to their impact on young listeners. Often, rewording is all that's needed to maintain meaning without introducing distractions.

Develop Your Testimony

A three-part outline of your life to prompt your testimony:

BC—before you became a Christian

The Cross—your conversion, the point you became a Christian

AD—your life after becoming a Christian

To help stimulate ideas for each era, write key words that come to mind when considering these questions:

BC

1. What were you like, personally and/or spiritually, before becoming a Christ-follower?

2. What caused you to begin considering a move toward God/Christ?

THE CROSS

1. What realization did you come to that finally motivated you to follow Christ?

2. Specifically, what did you do to become a Christian?

AD

1. How did your life begin to change after you began to follow Christ?

2. What are clear differences in your life now that you follow Christ, compared with your BC life?

Make Your Testimony Kid-Friendly

A three-part outline of your life to prompt your testimony:

BC—before you became a Christian

The Cross—your conversion, the point you became a Christian

AD—your life after becoming a Christian

Questions to consider that will help you filter your testimony through the four key communication dynamics:

BC

1. Is this a condition or lifestyle to which a child can relate? If no, then simplify.

2. Will a child be distracted by my sinful past or lifestyle details? If yes, then reword or delete.

THE CROSS

1. Is it clear that I took some action when I accepted Christ? If no, think more specifically.

2. Is what I did understandable and applicable to a child? If no, then reword.

AD

1. Is the change Christ made in my life easy to understand? If no, then describe the change differently, or focus on a different type of change.

2. Do I make description of my life as a Christian clear to a child? If no, then simplify by using words kids might say when they describe aspects of life.

The Four Components of the Gospel Message

adapted from *Becoming a Contagious Christian*

1. GOD

- He is a holy God, perfect in every way. Nothing else in this world fits the description of being perfect, so everything will fall short in a comparison to God. Yet, he created people to be like himself, along with an expectation of holiness or perfection.

  Be holy because I, the Lord your God, am holy.

  Leviticus 19:2

- He is a loving God, who loves each of us more than we can imagine. In fact, God created love.

  We love because he first loved us.

  1 John 4:19

- He is a just God, so he doesn't turn the other way and ignore sin.

  For I, the Lord, love justice, I hate robbery and wrongdoing.

  Isaiah 61:8 (NRSV)

2. Us

- All people commit sin. And when compared to God's beautiful standard of perfection, sin paints an ugly picture of a person.

  For all have sinned and fall short of the glory of God.
  Romans 3:23

- The debt each person accumulates from sin results in only one suitable payment, which is death—both physical and spiritual. This spiritual death is complete separation from God for eternity.

  For the wages of sin is death.
  Romans 6:23

- No matter how hard we try, we could never offer enough of a sacrifice to clear away all our sins. But someone has to.

  "The multitude of your sacrifices — what are they to me?" says the Lord.
  Isaiah 1:11

3. CHRIST

- Jesus Christ is God who became man and lived on earth.

  In the beginning was the Word, and the Word was with God, and the Word was God. . . . The Word became flesh and made his dwelling among us.
  John 1:1, 14

- Even though he never committed any sins, Christ died as our substitute—willfully punished for sins we commit. Following his sacrificial crucifixion came Christ's resurrection, which shows he has power over death. Christianity is faith in someone who still lives.

> *But God demonstrates his own love for us in this: While we were still sinners, Christ died for us.*
>
> Romans 5:8

> *I am the Living One; I was dead, and behold I am alive for ever and ever! And I hold the keys of death and Hades.*
>
> Revelation 1:18

- And Christ as our Savior offers us complete forgiveness for all our sins as a free gift.

> *For all have sinned and fall short of the glory of God, and are justified freely by his grace through the redemption that came by Christ Jesus.*
>
> Romans 3:23–24

> *For it is by grace you have been saved, through faith — and this not from yourselves, it is the gift of God.*
>
> Ephesians 2:8

4. You and Me

- The free gift of salvation must be accepted through a personal response to the gospel. We must ask Jesus into our heart as Lord and Savior, and the Leader of our lives.

> *That if you confess with your mouth, "Jesus is Lord," and believe in your heart that God raised him from the dead, you will be saved.*
>
> Romans 10:9

> *Be very careful, then, how you live — not as unwise but as wise. . . . Therefore do not be foolish, but understand what the Lord's will is.*
>
> Ephesians 5:15, 17

- At that moment, we become adopted into God's family.

  Yet to all who received him, to those who believed in his name, he gave the right to become children of God.
  John 1:12

- Because of Christ's presence in us, spiritual transformation takes place.

  Therefore, if anyone is in Christ, he is a new creation; the old has gone, the new has come!
  2 Corinthians 5:17

How to Effectively Reach a Young Child

Three areas of focus for deliberate, effective ministry to children in their early years:

POSITIVELY CONNECT A CHILD'S WORLD TO GOD

A connection between a person's surroundings and the Lord can serve as a strong starting point to reach someone to whom God seems unknown. To that end, create an association between kids' sensory experiences and God.

CLEARLY COMMUNICATE GOD'S TRUTH AND LOVE

Verbally communicate God's truth and love in tiny, bite-sized pieces through simple thoughts, plain words, and short sentences.

ACTIVELY REINFORCE THE MESSAGE

In addition to spoken words, actions and other nonverbal communication play key roles in introducing kids to God.

What Questions to Expect from Kids — Survey Results

Children wonder about more than they ask aloud. To keep informed of their questions, our ministry periodically surveys children to find out what they're thinking. The results of one such survey appear below, listed by topic in order of frequency. The range of topics and variety of questions reflects the breadth of this survey across hundreds of kids, some of whom accepted Christ years earlier—while other responses came from first-time church visitors.

QUESTIONS ABOUT THE BIBLE

When was the Bible made?
Who made the Bible?
Why was the Bible made?
What is the ark of the covenant?
Why does the Bible have two parts—and which one is more important?
How did God tell people what to put in the Bible?
What is in the book of Proverbs?
How many books are in the Bible?
Why does God talk to people in the Bible and not to me?
Why is it called the Bible?
What is the end of the world going to be like? And when is it going to happen?
Why aren't there more girls in the Bible?

Why are there other people besides God in the Bible?
Did Adam and Eve have a daughter or just sons?
Do I have to read the Bible every day?
Why are some Bibles different?

QUESTIONS ABOUT GOD

How can he make everyone, listen to everyone's prayers,
    and be everywhere at the same time?
Does God have a wife?
Why did God create Satan?
Why did he choose Mary to be Jesus' mother?
Why does God have so many names?

QUESTIONS ABOUT JESUS

Why was he killed?
How long did they spend crucifying him?
Was Jesus ever scared?
Why didn't people believe Jesus when he said he was the
    Son of God?
What happened to the people that died before Jesus came
    to earth?
Why did Judas turn Jesus in?
Why was Jesus Jewish?
Did Jesus have a girlfriend?
What kind of miracles did Jesus perform?

QUESTIONS ABOUT HEAVEN

Are there pets in heaven?

What is it like?

How many people are there?

Do you get tired singing all day long?

Is it fun to party every time someone becomes a forever friend with God?

Are the streets really made of gold—if so, how much money did it cost to make them all?

Do we get to ride up into heaven the same way Jesus did?

Are there dinosaurs in heaven?

Endnotes

Introduction

1. Quoted at Brainyquote.com, Copyright 2005 Xplore, Inc., *BrainyMedia.com* (February 8, 2005).

2. Jack W. Hayford, *Blessing Your Children: How You Can Love the Kids in Your Life* (Ventura, Calif.: Regal, 2002), 110.

Chapter 1 — The Game is One-on-One

1. George Barna, *Transforming Children into Spiritual Champions* (Ventura, Calif.: Regal, 2003), 33.

2. Karyn Henley, *Child-Sensitive Teaching* (Cincinnati, Ohio: Standard, 1997), 42.

3. James Strong, *Strong's Comprehensive Concordance of the Bible*, #5043 (Iowa Falls, Iowa: World Bible Publishers), 70.

4. James Dobson, response received by author from Focus on the Family website, *www.family.org* (July 8, 2004).

5. Joseph M. Stowell, *Why It's So Hard to Love Jesus* (Chicago: Moody Publishers, 2003), 90.

6. Billy Graham, quoted from the Billy Graham Evangelistic Association website, *www.billygraham.org* (August 4, 2004).

7. Bill Hybels, "Walk across the Room" (New Community message, Willow Creek Community Church, South Barrington, Ill., January 2004).

8. Gregory R. Suriano, ed., *Great American Speeches* (New York: Gramercy/Random House, 1993), 109.

Chapter 2 — Communicating with Kids

1. Suzette Haden Elgin, *The Gentle Art of Communicating with Kids* (New York: John Wiley & Sons, 1996), 9.

2. Red Auerbach quoted in Dr. John C. Maxwell, "Playing Over Their Heads," *Leadership Wired*, 7 no. 4 (3/12/04): *www.injoy.com* (March 12, 2004).

3. George Barna, *Transforming Children into Spiritual Champions* (Ventura, Calif.: Regal, 2003), 34.

CHAPTER 3 — SHARE YOUR STORY

1. Bill Hybels quoted in David Staal, "Mission Possible," *Children's Ministry Magazine* 12, September/October 2002, 68.
2. Bill Hybels, "Walk across the Room" (New Community message, Willow Creek Community Church, South Barrington, Ill., January 2004).
3. Bob Grimm, "Teaching Kids Is the Greatest Job in the World" (Breakout session, Promiseland Conference, Willow Creek Association, South Barrington, Ill., 2004).
4. Eugene Ehrlich and Marshall DeBruhl, *The International Thesaurus of Quotations*, 2nd ed. (New York: HarperCollins, 1996), 649.

CHAPTER 4 — SHARE GOD'S STORY

1. Craig Jutila, "The 'C' of Character" (General session 1, Purpose Driven Children's Ministry Conference, Saddleback Church, Lake Forest, Calif., April 2004).

CHAPTER 5 — THE PRAYER AND BEYOND

1. Karen L. Maudlin, "On the Family Front," *Christian Parenting Today*, (Winter 2003), 54.

CHAPTER 6 — WHAT IF I DON'T HAVE A STORY?

1. George Barna, "Number of Unchurched Adults Has Nearly Doubled Since 1991," *Barna Update*, Barna Research Group, *www.barna.org* (May 24, 2004).
2. C. Donald Cole, *How to Know You're Saved* (Chicago: Moody Publishers, 1988), 10.
3. Rick Warren, *The Purpose-Driven Life* (Grand Rapids, Mich.: Zondervan, 2002), 34.
4. Wayne Martindale and Jerry Root, *The Quotable Lewis*, #242 (Wheaton, Ill.: Tyndale, 1989), 120.
5. Shane Claiborne, "Faith for the 21st Century: Loving the Overlooked" (Axis weekend message, Willow Creek Community Church, South Barrington, Ill., 2001).
6. John Wooden, *Coach Wooden One-on-One* (Ventura, Calif.: Regal, 1996), Day 49.
7. Warren, *Purpose-Driven Life*, 120.
8. George Barna, *Transforming Children into Spiritual Champions* (Ventura, Calif.: Regal, 2003), 18.

9. Joseph M. Stowell, quoted in email message to author from Moody Bible Institute, November 11, 2004.

10. Martindale and Root, *The Quotable Lewis*, #1313, 523.

CHAPTER 7 — THE EARLY YEARS

1. Karyn Henley, *Child-Sensitive Teaching* (Cincinnati, Ohio: Standard, 1997), 43.

2. John T. Trent, Rick Osborne, and Kurt Bruner, *Teaching Kids about God: An Age-by-Age Plan for Parents of Children from Birth to Age Twelve* (Wheaton, Ill.: Tyndale, 2003), 5.

3. Adrian Rogers, *Future for the Family*, Love Worth Finding website, *www.lwf.org* (January 27, 2003).

4. Trent, Osborne, and Bruner, *Teaching Kids about God*, 21.

5. Henley, *Child-Sensitive Teaching*, 37.

6. Ibid.

7. Jack W. Hayford, *Blessing Your Children: How You Can Love the Kids in Your Life* (Ventura, Calif.: Regal, 2002), 49.

8. James Dobson, *Bringing Up Boys* (Wheaton, Ill.: Tyndale, 2001), 248.

9. Trent, Osborne, and Bruner, *Teaching Kids about God*, 13.

CHAPTER 8 — BIG DISCUSSIONS HAPPEN IN SMALL GROUPS

1. Rick Warren, *The Purpose-Driven Life* (Grand Rapids, Mich.: Zondervan, 2002), 130.

2. Betsy Taylor, *What Kids Want That Money Can't Buy* (New York: Warner, 2003), 138.

3. Craig Jutila, "The 'C' of Character" (General session 1, Purpose Driven Children's Ministry Conference, Saddleback Church, Lake Forest, Calif., April 2004).

4. Karyn Henley, *Child-Sensitive Teaching* (Cincinnati, Ohio: Standard, 1997), 71.

5. Henri J. M. Nouwen, *Here and Now* (New York: Crossroad, 1994), 95.

CHAPTER 9 — EXPECT QUESTIONS

1. J. S. Salt, *Always Kiss Me Goodnight—Instructions on Raising the Perfect Parent* (New York: Three Rivers, 1997), 48.

2. Eugene Ehrlich and Marshall DeBruhl, eds., *The International Thesaurus of Quotations* (London: Collins, 1996), 332.

3. George Y. Titelman, ed., *Random House Dictionary of Popular Proverbs and Sayings* (New York: Random House, 1996), 112.

4. David R. Veerman, et al., *101 Questions Children Ask about God* (Wheaton, Ill.: Tyndale, 1992), 2.

5. Betsy Taylor, *What Kids Want That Money Can't Buy* (New York: Warner, 2003), 95.

CHAPTER 10 — THE POWER OF EVERYONE

1. George Barna, "Evangelism Is Most Effective Among Kids," *Barna Update*, Barna Research Group, Ltd., *www.barna.org* (October 11, 2004).

2. "Think Big, Big Gift: Salvation," a lesson in the Promiseland Curriculum, Grade 2/3, *The Big Picture: God's Story from Genesis to Revelation*, (South Barrington, Ill.:Willow Creek Association, 2001).

3. Andy Stanley and Ed Young, *Can We Do That?* (West Monroe, La.: Howard, 2002), 56.

4. Northwoods Community Church, *www.nwoods.org* (February 19, 2005).

5. George Barna, *Turning Vision into Action.* (Ventura, Calif.: Regal, 1996), 38.

6. John Ortberg, "Parents and Kids: Same Planet, Different Worlds—Hearts and Souls" (Weekend message, Willow Creek Community Church, South Barrington, Ill., February 2003).

7. Stanley and Young, *Can We Do That?* 56.

FINAL WORD

1. Jack W. Hayford, *Blessing Your Children: How You Can Love the Kids in Your Life* (Ventura, Calif.: Regal, 2002), 152.

Index

children *(cont.)*
  belief without questioning,
      114–16
  belief without understanding,
      116–17
  and child-centered environment,
      173–76
  communicating God's love and
      truth, 119–22, 123–26
  communication with, 29–43,
      117–27, 185
  concept of love, 122
  Jesus' relationship with, 124
  ministry to, 195
  and parents' role in evangelism,
      23–27
  questions, 134, 197–99
  and self-worth, 135
  understanding of Gospels, 76
  value of stories, 36–38
Christ, 70
  relationship with, 105–7,
      110–11
  as Savior, 71, 192–93
Christians
  age of beginning relationship
      with Christ, 108
  becoming, 105–10
Claiborne, Shane, 106
Cole, Donald, 100
commitment, 170–71
communication
  with children, 29–43
  dynamics of, 31–42, 59–60, 185
  of God's love and truth, 119–22
  nonverbal, 125, 141
Commynes, Philippe de, 60
concrete language, 31–33, 72
conversion, 50–51, 53, 54
critical thought, 134
Cross, The (conversion), 50–51,
    53, 54

death, 70
details, stories, 39–40
direct response, 152–53
disbelief, 139
distractions, 40
Dobson, James, 21, 119–20
doubts, 139

Elgin, Suzette, 31
encouragement, 135
environment, child-centered,
    173–76
Ephesians
  2:8, 71, 193
  5:15, 17, 71, 193
evangelism, 23–27

faith, profession of, 99
fall, 136–38
familiarity, 171
filter, 59–60
1 Corinthians, 72
  2:1, 33
  9:20–23, 73
1 John
  4:19, 69, 191
1 Peter
  2:2, 126
  3:15, 134
1 Samuel
  1:21–28, 101
  3, 9, 103
  3:1–11, 102
  3:9, 106
four sentence testimony, 57–61,
    189–90
fun, 135–36, 175

Galatians
  1:13–17, 55–57
  1:23, 60

Leading Your Child to Jesus

How Parents Can Talk with Their Kids about Faith

David Staal

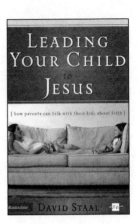

Although kids may hear about Jesus at church, parents need to know how to help their children make the most important decision of their lives. *Leading Your Child to Jesus* focuses on the core communication issues that enable parents to confidently engage kids in life-changing discussions. Moms and dads learn personal evangelism tools for sharing their own salvation story, explaining the gospel in language children understand, and starting a relationship with Jesus. Consistent with its companion book, *Leading Kids to Jesus*, this book uses stories from the book of Acts to provide a biblical foundation for key concepts. Application exercises prompt and prepare parents to put all the concepts into action. These kid-friendly communication principles have been proven through the experience of parents and from years of experience in Willow Creek Community Church's Promiseland children's ministry.

Softcover: 0-310-26537-1

Pick up a copy today at your favorite bookstore!

ZONDERVAN™

GRAND RAPIDS, MICHIGAN 49530 USA

WWW.ZONDERVAN.COM

Making Your Children's Ministry the Best Hour of Every Kid's Week

Sue Miller with David Staal

Promiseland is Willow Creek's highly successful children's ministry. Using examples from Promiseland and churches of all sizes around the country, this book provides step-by-step guidance and creative application exercises to help churches develop a thriving children's ministry—one that strives to be the best hour of every kid's week. Included are Scripture-based principles and practical resources for church staff members and volunteers who agree with the critical role children's ministry plays in a local church.

Making Your Children's Ministry the Best Hour of Every Kid's Week, based on twenty-eight years of experience at Willow Creek, explains four ministry foundations: Mission, Vision, Values, and Strategy.

Content includes detailed answers to questions facing every children's ministry:

- What does Jesus expect from children's ministry?
- How can we evangelize lost kids and disciple saved kids at the same time, and should we?
- How do we engage kids so they don't become bored?
- How do we get better at recruiting and leading volunteers?
- How can our ministry be a safe place for children?
- Six specific ministry values that address the needs of today's children
- Practical first steps for ministries that want to get serious about change
- Clear indicators of success in children's ministry

Softcover: 0-310-25485-X

WILLOW
Willow Creek Association

Willow Creek Association
Vision, Training, Resources for Prevailing Churches

This resource was created to serve you and to help you build a local church that prevails. It is just one of many ministry tools that are part of the Willow Creek Resources® line, published by the Willow Creek Association together with Zondervan.

The Willow Creek Association (WCA) was created in 1992 to serve a rapidly growing number of churches from across the denominational spectrum that are committed to helping unchurched people become fully devoted followers of Christ. Membership in the WCA now numbers over 10,500 Member Churches worldwide from more than ninety denominations.

The Willow Creek Association links like-minded Christian leaders with each other and with strategic vision, training, and resources in order to help them build prevailing churches designed to reach their redemptive potential. Here are some of the ways the WCA does that.

- **A2: Building Prevailing Acts 2 Churches—Today**—an annual two-and-a-half day event, held at Willow Creek Community Church in South Barrington, Illinois, to explore strategies for building churches that reach out to seekers and build believers, and to discover new innovations and breakthroughs from Acts 2 churches around the country.

- **The Leadership Summit**—a once a year, two-and-a-half-day conference to envision and equip Christians with leadership gifts and responsibilities. Presented live at Willow Creek as well as via satellite broadcast to over one hundred locations across North America, this event is designed to increase the leadership effectiveness of pastors, ministry staff, volunteer church leaders, and Christians in the marketplace.

- **Ministry-Specific Conferences**—-throughout each year the WCA hosts a variety of conferences and training events—both at Willow Creek's main campus and offsite, across the U.S., and around the world—targeting church leaders and volunteers in ministry-specific areas such as: evangelism, small groups, preaching and teaching, the arts, children, students, women, volunteers, stewardship, raising up resources, etc.

- **Willow Creek Resources®**—provides churches with trusted and field-tested ministry resources in such areas as leadership, evangelism, spiritual formation, spiritual gifts, small groups, stewardship, student ministry, children's ministry, the use of the arts-drama, media, contemporary music—and more.

- **WCA Member Benefits**—includes substantial discounts to WCA training events, a 20 percent discount on all Willow Creek Resources®, *Defining Moments* monthly audio journal for leaders, quarterly *Willow* magazine, access to a Members-Only section on WillowNet, monthly communications, and more. Member Churches also receive special discounts and premier services through WCA's growing number of ministry partners—Select Service Providers—and save an average of $500 annually depending on the level of engagement.

For specific information about WCA conferences, resources, membership, and other ministry services contact:

Willow Creek Association
P.O. Box 3188
Barrington, IL 60011-3188
Phone: 847-570-9812
Fax: 847-765-5046
www.willowcreek.com

We want to hear from you. Please send your comments about this book to us in care of zreview@zondervan.com. Thank you.

ZONDERVAN™

GRAND RAPIDS, MICHIGAN 49530 USA

ZONDERVAN.COM/
AUTHORTRACKER